REFORM OR DIE

REFORM OR DIE

Seven Women Theologians Speak

Laure Blanchon,
Isabelle de La Garanderie,
Véronique Margron, Anne-Marie Pelletier,
Lucetta Scaraffia, Anne Soupa,
and Marie-Jo Thiel

Paulist Press
New York / Mahwah, NJ

Scripture quotations are from New Revised Standard Version Bible: Catholic Edition, copyright © 1989, 1993 National Council of the Churches of Christ in the United States of America. Used by permission. All rights reserved worldwide.

Foreword translated from French by Nicolas Vodé
Chapter 2, "Lessons from the Abuse Crisis for Religious Life," translated from French by Claire Marre and Brigitte Minier
Chapter 5, "Renewing the Church by Following the Sense of the Faithful," translated from French with the assistance of Alice Pothron
Chapter 7, "One Church Can Hide Another," translated from French by Paulist Press

Cover image by Shyrokova/Shutterstock.com
Cover and book design by Lynn Else

Library of Congress Cataloging-in-Publication Data
Names: Blanchon, Laure contributor | La Garanderie, Isabelle de, 1985– contributor | Margron, Véronique contributor | Pelletier, Anne-Marie, 1946– contributor | Scaraffia, Lucetta, 1948– contributor | Soupa, Anne contributor | Thiel, Marie-Jo contributor
Title: Reform or die: seven women theologians speak / Laure Blanchon, Isabelle de La Garanderie, Véronique Margron, Anne-Marie Pelletier, Lucetta Scaraffia, Anne Soupa, Marie-Jo Thiel.
Other titles: Se réformer ou mourir. English
Description: Paperback. | New York : Paulist Press, [2025] | Summary: "This collection of essays by seven women theologians addresses issues of concern in today's Catholic Church"—Provided by publisher.
Identifiers: LCCN 2025015929 (print) | LCCN 2025015930 (ebook) | ISBN 9780809157730 paperback | ISBN 9780809189397 ebook
Subjects: LCSH: Catholic Church—Clergy—Sexual behavior | Church renewal—Catholic Church | Women in the Catholic Church | Church and the world | Church and social problems—Catholic Church
Classification: LCC BX1746 .S37713 2023 (print) | LCC BX1746 (ebook)
LC record available at https://lccn.loc.gov/2025015929
LC ebook record available at https://lccn.loc.gov/2025015930

ISBN 978-0-8091-5773-0 (paperback)
ISBN 978-0-8091-8939-7 (ebook)

Published by Paulist Press
997 Macarthur Boulevard
Mahwah, NJ 07430
www.paulistpress.com

Printed and bound in the
United States of America

CONTENTS

FOREWORD

"Like a boat about to sink, a boat taking in water on every side." These words are still famous, years after they were spoken by Cardinal Ratzinger at the Way of the Cross at the Colosseum on March 25, 2005, shortly after John Paul II's death. Using the classical imagery of the Barque of Saint Peter, the future pope Benedict XVI transparently expressed his concerns about the present state of the Church. Almost two decades later, one must recognize that the Church is struggling through a tempest of a violence seldom seen before, especially in Western countries such as France. After being weakened by our societies' secularization, the decrease in religious practice, dwindling priestly vocations, and disappearing institutions, the Church must now face the crises of sexual and spiritual abuse. Faced with such unfavorable conditions, many, even among Christians, are left wondering: Is there a future for the Church? How can it endure? How can one still hope, when everything points to "systemic" abuses, when words such as "terminal crisis" or even "implosion" are being used?

In this combination of deadly forces, it behooves us to remember the strong language of Deuteronomy, which still applies to our situation: "I have set before you life and death, blessings and curses. Choose life so that you and your descendants may live" (30:19). Throughout their history, the Church and the faithful have hearkened to these words and have risen again in the face of hardship. Through innovative solutions, bold reform, and brave initiatives, they have managed to allow the Gospel to be more than lifeless words. Although the challenges faced have varied across time, we can act in the same way today. We are indeed forced to choose: reform or die.

However, we will not be able to choose instantaneously, or by a pure act of will. When speaking of reform, we need reflection, discernment, dialogue, imagination, and competence. Thus, Éditions Salvator called for this book, soliciting the participation of seven female theologians. Avoiding both destructive pessimism and naïve optimism, they share their perspectives, contributing a foundational work based on biblical and theological as well as sociological and pastoral expertise.

This book opens with Lucetta Scaraffia's essay on the abuse crisis, especially abuses suffered by women, which have raised difficult questions about the Church's moral discourse and its relation to contemporary culture. Then Véronique Margron draws conclusions from these failings from her perspective on religious life, asking what frame it can offer for a healthy governance of power and service, affectivity and the Gospel's ideal, individual aspirations and the common good. Another sensitive question is the role women play in the Church. Anne-Marie Pelletier and then Marie-Jo Thiel address this issue, the former by analyzing ambiguities in common discourse on "feminine specificity," the latter in an effort to assign the proper place of women within Church institutions, drawing on biblical and theological perspectives. But advancing reform cannot be achieved only through authority; rather, it implies involving all the baptized and trusting the *sensus fidei* as defined by tradition. Isabelle de La Garanderie highlights this point, insisting on the synodal dimension envisioned by Pope Francis. Another emergency brought to the fore by Laure Blanchon is the place that is made, or not made, for the poorest, the most fragile within our communities. This is a sacred duty, all too often swept aside. Finally, in the last essay, Anne Soupa highlights how one Church can obscure another. How can requests currently being made for attention, inclusion, and inculturation be addressed? What paths must be opened so the Church can conform to the design for which it was created, to communicate the love given to all, bestowed upon us through Christ's death and resurrection?

These seven essays are invitations to dare to live out the Gospel in freedom, determination, and boldness, without fear of necessary, albeit rough, individual and collective conversions. It is now up to the readers to answer them.

Marc Leboucher
Editor, Éditions Salvator

PUBLISHER'S NOTE

Paulist Press is delighted to publish the English edition of this important book, *Reform or Die*, initially published in 2023 as *Se réformer ou mourir* by Éditions Salvator in France. Since the original publication, the papacy has passed from Pope Francis to Pope Leo XIV. While these are still early days for the new pope, much discussion has ensued about the legacy of Francis and whether and how Leo XIV will continue some of the important changes of Francis's papacy. Most significantly, how will Leo XIV respond to the priorities of women?

As such, this book and the radical choice that seven women theologians present in these pages now becomes even more poignant for the Church and the whole of society. Of course, any reform requires reflection, discernment, dialogue, imagination, competence, and commitment. The Church exercised these valuable tools through the Second Vatican Council and more recently through the papacy of Pope Francis in the form of synodality. From this synodal dimension emerge the authors' hope-filled approaches and contributions, drawing upon their biblical, theological, sociological, and pastoral experiences.

All these disciplines are needed, for the reform that is multilayered and multifaceted must be woven into a global socioeconomic and political fabric of diverse threads. These include various political systems, socioeconomic inequalities, the unequal burden of climate crises within and between countries in the North and South, ongoing conflicts, migration and displacement, and diverse cultures and religions, to name a few.

One solution will not fix everything. For this reason, ongoing reflection and discernment are paramount.

In his first address, Pope Leo XIV expressed his desire to build bridges, and he has been praised as a pastor who listens attentively to the needs of his flock. This volume is a call from seven competent theologians speaking out of their perceptions as women in the Church and society. It is more than just a call for reform; it is a call for discernment and mobilization of all the baptized—listening to the *sensus fidei*—to live and spread the gospel to which Christ calls each of us or else die as individuals and as a Church.

Paul McMahon
Publisher and President

ABBREVIATIONS

AL	*Amoris Laetitia* [On Love in the Family], Francis, March 19, 2016
CIASE	The French Independent Commission on Sexual Abuse in the Catholic Church
CL	*Christifideles Laici* [On the Vocation and the Mission of the Lay Faithful in the Church and in the World], John Paul II, December 30, 1988
CORREF	La Conférence des religieux et religieuses de France / The Conference of Men and Women Religious of France
DV	*Dei Verbum* [Dogmatic Constitution on Divine Revelation], Paul VI, November 18, 1965
EG	*Evangelii Gaudium* [The Joy of the Gospel], Francis, November 24, 2013
GE	*Gaudete et Exsultate* [Rejoice and Be Glad], Francis, May 19, 2018
ITC	International Theological Commission
LG	*Lumen Gentium* [Dogmatic Constitution on the Church], Paul VI, November 21, 1964
MD	*Mulieris Dignitatem* [On the Dignity of Women], John Paul II, August 15, 1988

1

COMMENTS FROM A CONCERNED CATHOLIC

Lucetta Scaraffia

I am a worried, anxious Catholic. I realize that this anguish—an anguish that devours me when I think and speak of the Church—is born precisely from my love for her, a love that I do not maintain as a duty but that I have discovered as a living and deeply rooted feeling in me, a love for a Church that I continue to consider as a Communion of Saints to which belong not only the living but also the many Christians who have preceded us, many of whom gave their life for her. Something of this old passion still speaks to me, something of these spirits who, in their time, were able to discern a divine work beyond the limits of the Church, and it prevents me from responding to my anguish with flight.

My anxiety comes from the fact that, despite the often superficial media successes of Pope Francis, the Catholic Church has fallen into a serious crisis. This crisis, of course, has roots in the past, but today it is more obvious and at an advanced stage, and it is very difficult to see an end to it. And, as was predictable, it has transformed into a general crisis of the religious dimension. "The reality of the missed encounter with God...transforms into despair in the face of the impossibility of meeting him,"

Hannah Arendt and Günther Anders write in their commentary on Rilke's *Duino Elegies*. And they affirm, by analyzing the condition of the religious dimension of their time in Europe, that "despair becomes the only vestige of religion."

A CHURCH IN CRISIS

External circumstances obviously contributed to the crisis of the Church: the broad decline of Christianity in the world, beginning with the European continent, and the crisis of Western European culture whose roots are deeply intertwined with the Christian tradition. In the West today, the Church must face a culture that is hostile to it. On the one hand, the disproportionate growth of individual rights—which goes so far as to include the right to have a child, the right to die, the right to change gender, the right for homosexual couples to build a regular family with children—dismantles the foundations of Christian morality. On the other hand, the refusal to recognize Christian roots is accompanied by an indiscriminate openness to other religions, partly out of fear of terrorist attacks. Such a cultural attitude denies the Christian identity.

Never has the Catholic tradition appeared more archaic, more outdated by its times and by the transformations of society. Today the voice of the pope, which in practice encapsulates that of the entire Church, rises only to invite mercy and welcome, and of course, peace, contributing to this state of affairs. We can undoubtedly approve of these exhortations, but they do not stand out much from those of the United Nations agencies and progressive movements.

From the Church, after the pontificate of Benedict XVI, we no longer receive a critical reading of modernity, nor a real confrontation with the changes that the world is experiencing. The only critical analysis of a contemporary phenomenon was the encyclical *Laudato Si'*, a severe critique of the destruction of our planet by human greed, which follows, however, in the wake of already existing environmental movements. And this happens while the moral and bioethical problems that contemporary society is forced to confront affect central aspects of the Christian worldview, on which the Church would therefore have a lot to say.

THE SEXUAL ABUSE SCANDAL

The reason for this silence, for this inability to look at the world from a Christian point of view, does not come from a cultural void but rather from a crisis of authority that leads to not opposing the dominant culture. We are currently experiencing a new and dramatic situation that has collapsed the trust we had in the priest as a witness to Christian values: the scandal of sexual abuse. A Church without credible witnesses can no longer make itself heard, even if its words are important and just.

The words of Jesus in the Gospel are clear: we recognize a tree by its fruits. This principle is also valid for institutions. What happens if we apply it to the Catholic Church? Sexual abuse of minors and nuns, which is concealed by hypocrisy, and which leads to other sins, such as abortions in the case of nuns, is not good fruit. This is not a question of a few bad apples but of a complex mechanism, installed for a long time to hide a reality that is particularly difficult to admit, namely, that chastity is only practiced by a minority of the clergy, while for other priests, transgressions, but especially abuses and their concealment, are the norm.

How can an institution in which hypocrisy reigns survive? One in which the members responsible for abuse show no interest in their victims? How can a Church survive that through its silences reveals that behind every sexual abuse lies a miserable reality, that of the abuse of power? A Church in which the clergy, through their abuse and cover-ups, consider themselves part of a higher class and show that they view other people as unworthy of respect and dignity?

This is a dramatic situation that causes people to lose all confidence, that destroys the respect that one could have had for the clergy, and that above all triggers a crisis of credibility so vast and so deep that almost all the statements coming from its representatives on sexual morality, but also morality in general, have lost all authority. The reason for this is simple: nearly all priests and members of the clergy, even if they were not directly responsible, were aware of certain abuses but turned a blind eye and remained silent. Many laypeople who did not want to lose the favor of the institution, which was still important and influential, are also complicit.

Seemingly to avoid directly confronting this problem, Pope Francis oriented his pastoral work on the old path, still practicable, of assistance to the poor. While a commitment worthy of praise, it neither erased nor put aside the other dramatic problems that continue to weigh on the Church's future, which depends on the way in which the problems are faced—or not. Not only the economically poor must be taken into account but also the victims of abuse and deception, who perhaps deserve even more compassion.

Can a religious institution maintain its moral authority when it severely condemns abortion in its sermons and then imposes it on nuns abused by priests to avoid scandal? The abuse of nuns may be even more serious and more scandalous than the abuse of minors. The very institution that condemns abortion and prohibits contraception tolerates them in the name of what is considered its most precious asset: its reputation, a reputation established, however, on lies and hypocrisy.

A pastoral ministry that aims to help the poor, the homeless, and the migrants forgets that the victims predisposed for sexual abuse mostly belong to the lowest category of the population. By an overwhelming majority, priests choose the poorest children as the objects of their vile attentions, children that perhaps belong to families helped by the parishes, and who are therefore hardly willing to oppose and denounce the priest. The poor are unfamiliar with lawyers and do not know how to seek justice.

As for the nuns, the social isolation in which they live makes the situation even more difficult. I have spoken with many sisters who have been abused; they are all women deprived of self-esteem, reduced to being human larvae, terrified. Sexual abuse has almost always been prepared for and accompanied by spiritual abuse that, for nuns, coincides with an abuse of power. The spiritual fathers, the confessors, and in the more modern version, the psychologist priests, take advantage of the opportunities given them by private meetings as a way to move on to sex, evoking the ancient gnostic conviction according to which the "perfect," that is to say, mystically superior beings, can transgress the moral laws.

How can we think that all this evil, tolerated and hidden, does not poison the entire Church, does not destroy its credibility forever? And yet the vast majority of the clergy continues to behave as if the first duty of the priest, but also of every Catholic, is to keep up at all costs a crumbling facade of imposture, to operate a system of power. It must be recognized that the complicity of those who hide the abuses is not only due to the fear of scandal but constitutes a strengthening of the system of power. "Man reinforces his own power more by lying rather than telling the truth," writes Luciano Manicardi.[1]

The first shock of this earthquake—which is not over and will have an even more serious phase when the scandal of the abuse of nuns and the abortions that were its consequence explodes definitively—damaged the image of the priest, associating even irreproachable and honest priests with this collapse. The trust with which the faithful turn to the priest and the habit of seeking advice from a priest for the various problems of life are tending to disappear.

While this distancing, or even just suspicion, may not reach the depth of one's faith, it undoubtedly undermines the trust that one can have in the Church. For a significant number of Catholics, this distrust of the Church leads to a distancing from religious practice and then, little by little, from faith itself.

The image of the priest crumbles all the more lamentably because in the past, it had been constructed and elevated into a sort of sacralization. We see this sacralization and a misplaced feeling of superiority in the paternalistic manner with which priests address laity in general and women in particular.

CELIBATE PRIESTS?

Today, the priestly role and mission must be completely reinvented. This scandal once again dramatically raises the subject of priestly celibacy. We all know that abuse also happens within families and is therefore perpetrated by married men, but the repeated transgressions on the part of priests of the rule of chastity—which by being concealed turns into abuse of the weakest—pose the problem urgently.

Accompanied by emotional solitude, celibacy can dry up the souls of those who should be even more attentive to the person than others. In this sense, the presence in a priest's life of a woman, in fact exercising control, can save him from the temptation of abuse. And even if sexual abuse is also present in families and in secular associations, as Pope Francis had often repeated, abuse constitutes a much more serious evil if committed by a priest. If the abuse comes from the one who should set a good example, the one who should help victims, who is left to defend the weak and care for them? If the one who presents himself as a man of God commits the abuse, what remains of the Christian religion?

UNRESOLVED QUESTIONS

Behind the problem of abuse lie the major unresolved questions in the Catholic tradition that are exploding in the face of modernity: the sexual question and the question of women. There is a crucial point that has never been resolved: behind the forms of modernization experienced without discernment, ancient heretical religious currents reappear, such as Gnosticism or Manichaeism, which should perhaps be studied in terms of their relationship with power.

Joseph Ratzinger was right when he wrote, in his last text

dedicated to abuse, that the increase in cases of abuse during the second half of the twentieth century can also be explained by the influence exerted by the sexual revolution, even within the Church. This is an assertion that has been widely criticized, but it is based on solid foundations. The Church did not know how to respond dialectically to the revolution in morals that took place during this period, and it hardened its traditional position, which considers that sexual relations are only acceptable inside marriage. The only cultural response came from Karol Wojtyla who, in his book *Love and Responsibility*, highlighted the spiritual force of the sexual bond between spouses, seeking in this way to overcome the demonization of sex present in the Catholic tradition. But that was too little.

At the same time, the winds of the sexual revolution reached Catholic communities. Today, the majority of couples who marry in the Church arrive at marriage after having lived together for several years and often even after the birth of their children. How could we think that this wind of freedom has not also affected the clergy and religious? How could we think that Wilhelm Reich's widely shared theory, according to which the absence of a happy sex life, summed up in the myth of the orgasm, causes neuroses and sadness, did not also provide justification to the clergy? But since this problem was not addressed by the hierarchy, except in a repressive manner, it was resolved clandestinely by seeking weak subjects who guaranteed silence.

The protection provided by the concealment of this type of transgression was ensured by a well-rooted Catholic custom, which consisted of always defending the good reputation of the institution even to the detriment of the truth and, above all, the condemnation of the guilty party. This custom, as we have seen, worked very well. It even grew stronger in the postwar years; perhaps the bishops agreed with Reich and feared having neurotic priests? Public opinion, moreover, has always been—and even more so under the influence of the sexual revolution—disposed to forgive sexual sins and to consider them in a certain sense as inevitable.

During my research on the history of the Church conducted in ecclesiastical archives, I have repeatedly come across investigations from past centuries devoted to priests who had had relationships with their servants, but also with some parishioners, relationships often tolerated by the husbands. These were relationships in which the dimension of power was very present, but which generally seemed to take place between consenting adults. In the last decades of the twentieth century, this type of woman became rare; those who engaged in consensual relationships with priests ended up demanding marriage, children, and recognition. They no longer accepted subordinate or clandestine roles. How to engage in clandestine sex was resolved by turning to subordinate subjects, forced to silence by their weakness, thus minors and nuns.

The ecclesiastical institution has never concerned itself with possible victims, but only with warning and saving the guilty. According to the totally macho conception of sexual relations such as that of Catholic culture, any type of sexual relations creates a certain pleasure; thus, the victim is also believed to betray the sixth commandment. The victim is seen as an accomplice, without us knowing to what extent this was involuntary.

A striking example of this aberration is given to us by the Rupnik affair, which recently broke. More than twenty sisters accuse this religious artist of sexual abuse and abuse of power, but the Congregation for the Doctrine of the Faith condemned him, a conviction later removed by the pope himself, only because, as a confessor, he absolved the nuns he had abused of their sin against the sixth commandment.

The Question of Sexuality

These are the most terrifying aspects of abuse; these are the conditions that allow and favor its repetition. As long as the Church does not confront the sexual question with honesty and courage, as long as it does not erase the halo of impurity with which it has surrounded all aspects of the sixth commandment, it will not be able seriously to come to terms with this scandal.

An example showing how this situation poisons all pastoral care relating to the body and sexual behavior is the case of Tony Anatrella, renowned psychoanalyst, ideologist of the Catholic reaction to the homosexual liberation movement, then a priest himself convicted of sexual violence. Some of the official documents of the Church, including the reference book *Lexicon. Termini ambigui e discussi su famiglia, vita e questioni etich* (Lexicon of Ambiguous and Controversial Terms: On Life, the Family, and Ethical Questions), have drawn their inspiration from his texts. Even after his double life was discovered, the texts remained. They were not reexamined in the light of what happened, and there was no self-criticism.

How can we not see that with such attitudes, the true and deep reasons, anthropological and biblical, that support the Christian vision of sexuality are no longer perceptible? Those who choose to present these reasons with competence and serenity seem to be saying something extraordinary, something ultimately new and revealing, whether we agree with them or not. For example, this is how one feels when reading the recent *Pastoral Letter on Human Sexuality* from the bishops of Scandinavia, who dare to approach the question with realism but without forgetting Christian tradition:

> It is a giant step, for example, to move from multiple relationships to a life as a faithful couple, whether or not this faithful relationship fully corresponds to the objective criteria of a sacramentally blessed union. Any quest for integrity is worthy of respect and deserves to be encouraged. Growth in wisdom and virtue is organic. It happens gradually. At the same time, this growth, to be fruitful, must move towards a goal. Our mission and task as bishops is to indicate the direction of the path of Christ's commandments, which is a path of peace and life. It is narrow at the starting point, but it widens as you progress. We would be failing in our duties towards you [the bishops write to their faithful] if we offered you less

than that. We were not ordained to preach our own little ideas.[2]

Listening to Women

The issue of women, who in Catholic communities are neither respected nor listened to, is linked to the sexual one. In practice, we refuse to recognize women's full humanity. In fact, the sexual question has only been examined from the male point of view; an innate distrust of women has led men to imagine them more as temptresses than as possible victims. The idea that one can experience pleasure during abuse is born from a male prejudice, but it influences the entire understanding of sexuality in the Catholic Church. Since the sixteenth century, "thou shall not commit adultery" of the sixth commandment has turned into "you shall not commit impure acts." Pleasure became a danger to the purity of the believer's soul. Physical impurity, which Jesus had erased from the lives of Christians, thus returns in this form.

A profound revision of this view of sexuality is therefore essential to allow the Church to emerge from the scandal of abuse. This must include the voices of women, who have never been listened to.

The oppression of women in the ecclesiastical institution, the little consideration they enjoy in the life of the Church, and the poorly concealed contempt with which they are viewed by the clergy are certainly not new. This sad situation was denounced by Hildegard of Bingen in the twelfth century and by Teresa of Ávila in the sixteenth century, to cite only two examples.

But the feminist revolution of the twentieth century has in a way besieged the Church. The merciless comparison between what is happening in Western society and the internal stagnation specific to the institutional Church, especially with regard to women, has made the situation untenable. The problem of the priesthood, which has always been refused to women, is only the tip of a patriarchal system that does not listen to the female voices present within it, that does not respect women and, even less, nuns, and that survives by raising barriers intended to prevent women from truly participating in the life of the Church.

The Gospel Revolution

How can we change the status of women? How can we free women from this inferiority without literally reproducing the secular model? On this question, the Church must draw inspiration from its most ancient tradition by carrying out the revolution that the Gospel began and that centuries of patriarchy then nearly but not entirely extinguished. The seeds of true equality between men and women preached by Jesus have fructified in secular society, precisely thanks to its Christian roots. This is why female emancipation is so difficult to export outside of these Christian-based societies.

But this evangelical achievement escaped the hands of the Church and took paths unacceptable for Christian morality with the claim of abortion as a right, for example, or even the negation of sexual difference. If the Church had had the courage to reconnect with its own origins and to rethink the role of women within it, it would have acquired the credibility necessary to propose a Christian feminism, a critical feminism on issues such as abortion or sexual freedom, highlighting, above all, the price that women pay under the effect of these libertarian assertions. In this way, Western societies were almost completely deprived of a critical look at feminism as it developed, or else these critiques remained the heritage of an intellectual elite.

Let us also think about the drop in the birth rate, mainly due to women giving birth to their first child much later, at an age when conception becomes more difficult if not impossible despite the use of assisted procreation. This situation is often due to the lack of information on the real risks of this continual postponement but also to the sexual freedom that does not encourage young men who are not subject to a biological clock to assume family responsibilities while they are young.

So much information is suppressed so as not to taint the myth of sexual freedom presented as the guarantee of happiness.

The Church could offer a discourse on the limits of the utopia of the sexual revolution. But Catholic culture is distracted; it looks elsewhere, and it does not even realize that, while Catholics no longer dare to publicize natural methods of birth control, ecological movements defend them by denouncing the contraceptive pill as one of the reasons for world pollution.

Deeper Problems

All questions concerning the rules of sexual behavior refer to deeper problems, such as the meaning of human life, the relationship between the soul and the body and between the human being and nature. But nothing is said on these points either.

It would seem that after having confined itself for years to a rigid and unconvincing defense of traditional morality unnecessarily "spiritualized" by John Paul II, the Church has today thrown in the towel and no longer wants to intervene. It completely lacks a sense of responsibility in the face of the transformations of contemporary society, the scandal of abuse, and major unresolved questions.

This collapse has erased the prestige of the Church as a moral agency and has rendered worthless any reflection or criticism on the part of Catholics on the major themes of bioethics that run through today's world. Any recourse to Christian tradition in the face of the great dilemmas that distress human beings has been discredited: the fear of death, the dilemma of suffering, and more generally, the difficulty of finding meaning in one's life. The critical dimension of faith has been lost and deprived of any possibility of action for the future.

This should not be so; it would be preferable to separate the great Catholic tradition from the scandals of today, but we cannot forget that a religious tradition, a worldview, is transmitted mainly by its witnesses. Not everyone is willing or able to seek answers in the treasury of Christian thought, but the example of its adherents is accessible to all and immediately understandable.

Beyond the scandals, we constantly see Catholics chasing notoriety and following the modernization of the means of communication, as if we could fight against the problem of the decline in religious practice by intervening on the networks of social media or on television with means that are more like advertising than like Christian witness. Volunteering, social commitment, and Church outreach are undoubtedly positive realities, but they do not answer existential questions, especially in a society that cannot avoid asking them, although society no longer believes that after death the good are rewarded and the evil are punished. Nor do they help us to find the alternative wisdom of how to think of the world that is the heart of the Gospels.

For this reason, the search for spirituality, for answers to life's deepest questions, increasingly takes paths other than those offered by Christian tradition.

In this regard, the success enjoyed for decades now by a great mystic, Simone Weil, who always remained on the threshold of conversion to Christianity, a threshold that she nevertheless did not cross, is significant. Her journey is a perfect example of deep spirituality, but without faith. This explains the basic reason for its success: spirituality is what contemporary people first seek, while faith distances them and fills them with distrust.

Martin Buber says it well in his book *Eclipse of God*. Today the human being "does not deny a transcendent God: quite simply, he does without it," because "it is not God that 'modern conscience' hates, but it is faith."[3]

OPENING DOORS TO HOPE

If it is inevitable that this world dissuades human beings from seeking meaning in their lives, the task of the Church is to give them the possibility of finding it. This is not to suggest that people lead a life projected outward without asking fundamental questions, ignoring the mystery of our existence, the sovereign opportunity of the human race.

Therefore, the problem of the Church today is not so much to overcome the divide between progressives and conservatives—it is not a question of ecclesiastical politics—but of returning to its spiritual roots and of making lives match its words.

As in the Old Testament during the crossing of the desert, the Hebrew people advanced from illusion to disillusion, today we laypeople, men and women together, must act to interrupt this repetitive and short-lived mechanism by opening the doors to hope. Not hope as a feeling but as a responsibility and a task that opens onto a future. In this renewal, part of the previous form dies and is lost, for rebirth is not a version of the past but instead is something new.

2

ESSENTIAL LESSONS FROM THE ABUSE CRISIS FOR RELIGIOUS LIFE

Véronique Margron

How can we talk about the dynamics of reform in the Church if the abuse crisis is not carefully considered? Can we fail to see that ways of operating have been called into question through the report of the Independent Commission on Sexual Abuse in the Catholic Church (CIASE) in France that has made the many scandals come at last to light? Various works published in 2023 also pointed at the need to rethink religious life and the place of our respective spiritual traditions.

A CALL FOR VIGILANCE

The first lesson to be learned from the tragedies and crimes of abuse is a powerful call to vigilance. The systemic nature of the abuses must be matched by systemic watchfulness, both for the instructors of young religious men and women and for all those who exercise responsibilities in communities, such as superiors or priors. The modes of governance are the primary concern here; do they leave enough room for otherness and plurality? At a time when the Church as a whole, particularly under the impetus of Pope Francis, once again put forward synodality, let us not forget that religious life is—or at least should be—structurally synodal. Through various structures (councils, chapters, elections, and so forth), it bears witness to practices marked by collegiality and the search for consensus to develop common orientations and make decisions. Much has been highlighted of the excesses in the "new communities" lately—unfortunately, rightly enough—but how can we explain that despite these institutional safeguards, historical religious communities have also experienced and continue to experience abuses, whether under the form of an attack on freedom of conscience or critical thinking, or abuse of power or sexual violence?

Here stands the fragility of religious life in France today. There are certainly procedures at work to limit leaders' terms of office and bodies to regulate power, but when we can no longer find the people to take on responsibilities, when the succession of a superior is unthinkable because we cannot appoint someone competent to replace him or her, what can we do? The people in question are not necessarily abusers, but the weakness of the institution means that they can become abusers. The same people will be asked to run the structure, and mandates will simply be exchanged without any real renewal. This is not so much a case of clericalism but a form of corporatism, of *entre-soi* that can only encourage the inflation of power or abuses of authority. Yet to counter such excesses, we clearly need a sufficiently strong and structuring body of institutions. All too often, if we fail to look at these situations of weakness, if we fail to consider the measures that need to be taken, such as mutual aid, external support, or even the regrouping of certain communities, we find ourselves in a deadlock. There is a risk of blindness in the face of reality, often for reasons that are too quickly based on spiritual generosity and abandonment to

Providence. This can lead to abuses of all kinds relating to obedience, isolation, and forms of secrecy in the name of necessary "discretion."

This vigilance must be exercised regarding external and internal abuses. Thus, reforming our practices and structures does not mean revolutionizing everything but at least revisiting them so that they can be better adapted to prevent the tragedies that are being disclosed. This is undoubtedly the cornerstone of the change we need to make. We will lose a lot on the evangelical level if we do nothing in this direction.

QUESTIONING RELIGIOUS LIFE AND THE VOWS

As a second lesson, we need to question our theological vision of religious life itself and the way we talk about it. Since Vatican II, the intuition that religious life rests first and foremost on the unfolding of the sacrament of baptism has become widely accepted. To use an expression coined by Patrick C. Goujon, SJ, by making profession, we commit ourselves to "living our baptism intensely." Such dynamics of the Christian life, shared in different ways by all the baptized in the Church, form the basis of the vows of chastity, poverty, and obedience. Then, according to the founder or foundress and the type of spirituality they refer to, each institute or congregation will put forward a specific understanding of the vows. In Dominican spirituality, for example, the vow of obedience incorporates the other two vows (chastity and poverty). Similarly, the vow of stability, for monastic orders, includes these vows.

But with the phenomenon of abuse and sexual aggression, this beautiful ideal of intense evangelical life can be turned inside out. When in a position of responsibility, leaders can easily manipulate members by claiming a vow of obedience to pressure them to get what they want, including the worst, as so many dreadful testimonies have shown. The best of intentions, at least at first glance, can turn into a perverse situation.

We tend to think of the emotional and sexual abuses that have occurred in connection with the vow of chastity, but other types of abuse can be generated by a misguided practice of the vow of poverty, by depriving a person of any means of autonomy, or by forcing them into forms of begging or dependence.

Because of this, we need to be circumspect when we speak of religious life as "radical" or as a testimony to "the Absolute of God." What would we not do in the name of a so-called absolute, whether religious or political, as we have seen tragically enough in the course of history in all sorts of ideologies, totalitarian ideals, or sects? We should also be careful with the vocabulary that evokes religious life in terms of a "perfect life." Christ in the Gospel does invite us to "be perfect, therefore, as your heavenly Father is perfect" (Matt 5:48), but we must never forget that the word "as" in theology means an analogy, implying a distance and not a mimicry. Nor should we forget that in Luke 6:36, we must be "merciful, just as your Father is merciful." Considering evangelical life as an ideal and therefore impossible to attain can only generate ambiguity and unease in people who will necessarily feel unworthy or imperfect in front of such elevated goals. This feeling of imperfection, or even shame, makes them ideal prey for a manipulator.

If we look more concretely at the life and workings of religious life, the evangelical counsels—the three vows of chastity, poverty, and obedience—can clearly be used for illicit power. Consider the young religious who makes his or her profession before the superior with the formula "Into your hands, I promise...." This magnificent sign of availability and trust can later be recalled by the superior to justify excessive, even unfair and inhuman injunctions.

In the same way, emphasizing "discipleship" can also prove to be an ambiguous attitude. Every confessing Christian wishes to be seen as a disciple of Christ, and no one can be self-instituted. Anthropological reality shows that, whoever we are, we need teachers, consciously or unconsciously, to constitute ourselves as we are, to grow, to identify ourselves, and to set ourselves apart. But there can be a fine line between being a free disciple and a submissive pupil. Religious and mystical manipulation can easily unfold in the case of a young person who commits to religious life with all the generosity of his or her heart and being. During this magnificent and overwhelming process of self-giving, when committing oneself to following Christ with others within a desired and admired community, putting aside one's own critical spirit is quite normal. It is then up to the community to be watchful for two so that the freedom, the integrity of being, and the conscience of the person who wants to follow in our footsteps should be preserved. The superior, the mentor, and the institute itself are all disciples of the unique master that Christ is, a master who is also a friend, a companion, and a servant. Otherwise, if the community and its representatives claim to know God's will for the other person, the manipulation of language makes it easier to enslave people, like the fly caught in a spider's web. From the outside, no one may be aware of it; the system sounds legitimate, even holy, when in fact it is devastating and false.

The terrifying effects can be seen in many concrete situations. This was the case with the sisters of the Community of Saint John who were abused by Marie-Dominique Philippe and others. A nun was encouraged to lie to canonical visitors who had come to listen to the sisters of the community after critical reports of misconduct. She justified herself by saying, "In any case, our Mother knows what is good for us." Shaming sisters when they complained or asked questions about acts of violence against them, their superior used to answer, "Sister, you have to carry your cross. You don't know how lucky you are to be accompanied by the Father."

Another tactic uses a hellish circle of contradictory injunctions in which gratifications unpredictably alternate with punishments and humiliations, contributing to the inner destruction of the self, including sisters' identity, their reason, and their own clear-sightedness, by blowing hot and cold. This is well described in Anne-Charlotte de Maistre's book *Liturgies sous Prozac*, which recounts her time in the Monastic Fraternities of Jerusalem (Salvator, 2022), or in *Le Silence de la vierge*, by

Marie Laure Janssens (Bayard Adulte, 2017). At times, the young "recruit" is complimented, praised for her dynamism and generosity, and even sent abroad on foundation missions. At other times, she is told that she is worthless, that she only thinks of herself, or that she listens too much to herself when the first signs of nervous breakdown appear. The trap then closes on the gift of radicalism. Only outside intervention can—perhaps—rescue the victims.

THE AUTONOMY OF THE INDIVIDUAL

Adjusting our understanding and practice of the evangelical counsels brings to light a third lesson: in our communities, what place do we give to the autonomy of the individual? If the vows do not contribute to the growth of the individual, with his or her freedom of conscience and inner freedom, what is the point of claiming them and putting them into practice?

We face a new challenge today: how can we stop placing in opposition the autonomy of the individual with the quest for the common good, the common life, and all that it requires in terms of compromise, mutual effort, and renunciation? This is not self-evident in today's mindset, and finding agreement between these two demands remains difficult, but such tension can be stimulating. Opposing the two poles rigidly may be critical; we'd rather find a new way to pursue the same goal, the evangelical life, together.

In a society marked by individualism, governance is not easy. Young people enter religious life at a later age and have often developed habits of autonomy. It becomes more difficult to ask a sister or a brother to do something or to take on responsibilities without being told, "You're infringing on my freedom!" It is no longer unusual to be accused of abuse of power. But questioning may be good, and it is always worth doing. There is no recipe for dealing with such dilemmas; we must cope with them. At the very least, the exercise of authority must involve a genuine dialogue in which we work together to find the best possible solution without too many presuppositions. This humble and modest path, in the simplicity of everyday conversation, is a form of deliberative ethics that is magnificent in its very humanity. No one is the master of truth; there is only one master, friend, and servant who must be followed.

The articulation between the common good and the autonomy of the individual is perhaps even more acute in contexts in which being a religious means enjoying a certain social and religious status. Many religious administer colleges, schools, and care facilities, or have pastoral responsibilities. What happens when they feel out of place, exhausted, or on the verge of a burnout? Leaving religious life would mean abandoning their religious-social status. Not living in the guise of an external identity is always a work in progress.

At the same time, I am convinced that a healthy obedience can sustain our existence and allow us to develop authentically as a person. It reminds us that we are not "self-made entrepreneurs" but that we receive ourselves from an Other and from others. It reiterates that listening, conversation, and the search for the best give everyone the chance of a better life. We must absolutely encourage a fair and human vision of obedience, as opposed to any spirit of submission that is unhealthy because it is childish. I remember a terrible sentence from a sister when faced with what was asked of her: "I want to do what the superior wants because it is the will of God. Now I have to get my humanity to follow." Could we eventually believe that there is a relationship between God's desire and human desire, between the common good and the good of each individual? Not without tension, not without struggle, and even with heartbreak, but without dissociation.

Some time ago, the psychoanalyst Marie Balmary warned us about the way in which a religious ideal may or may not encourage spiritual growth. The religious way of being, especially the training, may be seen as a mold that one must adapt to, even if it means being broken. This risks breaking the originality and singularity of the individual, thwarting his or her chance to sound his or her own particular note on the path to the Gospel. On the other hand, we believe that training is a womb, the environment in which a being can unfold, like a child in its mother's womb. We must deal with two singular living beings.

As part of our training activities, we should not hesitate to ask ourselves: what room do we leave for people's creativity? We ask not to let everyone do as they please, but to put into practice a community, with places and roles for each member, that lives from the Spirit of Christ and wishes to put the Gospel into practice, according to the unique story and specific color of a tradition.

LISTENING TO THE VOICES OF THE VICTIMS

Our fourth important lesson, which we could have dealt with first, is the absolute need to listen to the voices of the victims. To insist on this dimension is not to be fascinated by evil. Being present and listening to broken people is inherent in the Church and in the vocation of religious life being true to the Gospel. The theology of Jean-Baptiste Metz has considerably developed this dimension. But what is special here is that the victims are of and within the Church itself. Not only are they victims of male abusers—some of them predators—but they are also victims of the Church and its institutions, which have denied and covered up these abuses and aggressions.

Once again, we are brought back to the roots of religious life, which is nothing other than following in the footsteps of Christ as much as we can. Listening to the victims means, in the most obvious sense, placing ourselves at the foot of the cross of Christ. Jesus was crucified by his own people, by the crowd and the chief priests, just like the people who are victims of those who should have been looking after them. For us, this presence and this listening are not a morbid fascination for the suffering of others but a way of affirming that the only true place is where Christ dies, the place where life flows, through the blood and water that gush from his pierced side. In other words, the issue of abuse is not an issue like any other; it is a huge, serious, and crucifying tragedy that brings us back to the truth of our life choices. The way we see the world and religious life can never be the same again. There is an irrevocable and irreversible dimension to this.

This special listening is not simple neutrality. Such wounds are, for us, too, a blow, a necessary test for religious life. How can we imagine remaining neutral when we are affected ourselves? Not because we want to pretend we feel what the victims are going through, but because our common humanity demands that our own flesh, our faith, and our very existence should be affected. So perhaps we become "witnesses of witnesses" whose lives will no longer be as they were.

The fact that religious men and women have been abused and assaulted cannot leave us unmoved in our life as followers of Christ. What sense can religious life have if it does not fight so "that the world may be saved" (John 3:17)? We are present to the victims who have been plunged into the abyss by their assaulters so that they can be restored as much as possible into their integrity, their freedom, and their trust. The urgency to restore this evangelical obligation must powerfully spur us in our way of being and doing and in our courage. It takes us back to the intensity of baptismal life that we mentioned at the beginning.

Listening unconditionally to the victims shows the reality of our insolvent debt to them. Taking incarnation and proximity seriously is at the heart of every Christian life, every religious life. As I am saying this, I remember meeting victims who had undertaken a restoring process initiated by the commission chaired by Antoine Garapon. It took place where unthinkable acts of sexual violence had occurred, in a school run by the Brothers of Saint Gabriel, where a sadistic sexual predator used to perpetrate his evil doings. He may have assaulted 150 children, boys and girls, ages seven or eight. The brothers, together with the members of the commission and a group of around forty victims, carried out a very thorough investigation, a very courageous work of truth, the kind that hurts and plunges into the abyss those who discover the reality of who their fellow brother was and the deeply failed approach of the congregation during all those years. The group had organized a memory day attended by their relatives and friends, other victims, people from the village, the civil authorities (mayor, member of parliament) and the religious authorities (bishop). On that day, these women and men showed how much this "murder of the child they were, thus killing the adult in them" had meant for their lives. But they also showed how they had become not only witnesses but also actors in their own restoration through the work they had done with the brothers today and the Garapon Commission. Recognition had made legal compensation and restoration possible. On that day, *they* were the actors in relationship and friendship. Those whose trust and intimate ties had been destroyed could now revive meaning, direction, and orientation, giving another taste, at last, to their existence.

I deeply believe that religious life must learn from these women and men, and from all their companions in misfortune, not to change everything but to allow ourselves to be touched by this very concrete truth: what makes us human?

Perhaps this also gives us a glimpse of an essential dimension of apostolic religious life, particularly when it means being as close to people as possible, without any particular role or hierarchy, journeying together in the same boat. We have probably forgotten it because it is no longer part of the landscape, but the figure of the religious caretaker, teacher, or catechist, at the service of others, without distinction, means genuine support and sharing people's lives. We cannot lose sight of the flexibility and plasticity of the forms of religious life. All of us must question ourselves when our lifestyles and positions set us at a distance from the common reality. Religious life does not mean being in a superior or an all-knowing position. Our skills and qualifications are not titles of glory but an indispensable way of taking people seriously in order to advocate for the most vulnerable.

WHAT ABOUT OUR SPIRITUAL TRADITIONS?

All religious traditions are affected by the scandal of sexual abuse and assault, the so-called new communities as well as those from great lineages: St. Benedict, St. Francis, St. Dominic, St. Ignatius, the French School, and the like. No one is immune from perversion. After the 2021 assembly, the Conference of Men and Women Religious of France (La Conférence des religieux et religieuses de France—CORREF) set up, among other things, working groups[1] on governance and on the "weaknesses and resources" of our traditions. The aim was to look at how our rules of life and their interpretations could lead to abuse or, on the contrary, be antidotes. We all have this reading and rereading to do. Manipulation is always exercised through what appears to be the "highest," the most noble, the most radical. The best can then become the worst.

For example, how can we flush out the paternalism, even feminine paternalism, that can be exercised in communities, especially when one of the members is a "father" or a "mother"? The vocabulary we use is significant. The names of "superior," of "supreme moderator," and even "families," which implies parents and children, are fraught with ambivalence or, at the very least, ambiguity. Language can easily be the gateway to manipulation. But for St. Benedict, if the abbot is indeed a father, there are only brothers and not sons. How can we dismantle the concentration of power—or the abdication of personal responsibility—when the community is always told that "it's up to the superior"? How can we refuse to be in a position that quickly becomes one of prestige and impunity because we are "men or women of God"?

In the Ignatian tradition, we are familiar with the famous *Perinde ac cadaver*, obeying as a corpse would, which "allows itself to be led anywhere and treated any way" (Constitution 547). The demand is inordinate and could justify any abuse of power. It even verges on blasphemy since it places the superior in the position of God. But Ignatius himself makes it clear that nothing can be demanded in the name of obedience that would be a sin. What an incredible safeguard against abuse! So, neither judgment nor conscience can be abolished, quite the contrary. And how can we fail to recall that the same Ignatius insisted on the meaning of a relationship with God "like a friend with his friend"? This space, then, is not of subjection but of parity and freedom.

Finally, it is worth remembering that God takes no pleasure in anyone's death, as Ezekiel reminds us (18:32). Authority in religious life commits us to the conversion of our images of God and of our interpersonal relationships.

Let's not equivocate; the established authority should have real power. If not, the door is open to other abuses. How else can authority influence reality? The crisis has also revealed that some authorities are powerless to act. Their power has its own limits: those set by the rules, the constitutions, the mode of governance, and so on.

This relationship between authority and power is essential. For if we claim that authority is simply "a service," as is so often said in the Church, we run the risk of no longer being able to challenge it. In fact, being a servant is unlimited; the only Master, Christ, gave his own life.

But then, how can you dare to disagree with your superior? Here again there is a reversal that can prove perverse. Many founders who have become predators have played on their image as "great servants" detached from the desire for power.[2] If need be, they pretended to withdraw, while, at the same time, they kept on imposing their lead by manipulating people and taking pride in pseudo-spiritual teachings.

Some will also use the words of Christ in the Gospel: "I do not call you servants any longer...I have called you friend" (John 15:15). But let us not forget that in saying this, Jesus clearly instituted the Twelve with powers to heal the sick and cast out demons. If someone exercises authority with the necessary power, they can obviously experience it as a service. But it does have its own outlines: duration of office, objects, conditions of exercise. Recognition of these conditions is precisely what can enable things to change.

AVENUES FOR REFORM?

After this nonexhaustive review of the lessons to be learned from the crisis of sexual abuse from the perspective of religious life, can we sketch out avenues for reform?

Rather than "reform or die," I would rather say, "die or reform" and even "die, and then reform." To truly reform ourselves in this context that has led children, women, and men to be shattered and sometimes destroyed by religious people and the complacency of institutions means to die to deadly practices.

The systemic nature of abuses must be matched by systemic reforms and transformations. Practices that destroy freedom, conscience, and integrity must disappear for reform to become possible and credible.

The paschal mystery is at the heart of our life. It constantly brings us face-to-face with the reality that, for life to be transmitted, we must consent to death. It is up to us, to each institute, to look at what detrimental ways of being and doing need to die.

Then, there is a second way of thinking that says that if we do not change, then indeed, we are going to die, including dying while we are still breathing! In France, many of our institutes have a high average age; this is a reality, not a problem. You can be old and still alive! And even, as we say in palliative care, one can die while still very much alive. But if we do not change, we die before our time. There is no alternative. And to transform ourselves is to risk uncertainty and possible failure. But there is no other way. "Choose life so that you may...live" (Deut 30:19) is not a self-evident statement but a risky call to be alive thanks to our choices and directions.

In many cases, we have discovered that admired and even adulated founders and foundresses have turned out to be the originators of abuse. For some institutes, the temptation was great to have them canonized by the Church soon after their death, in the name of the "many fruits" they had produced. We know that under the pontificate of John Paul II, in a laudable desire to show that holiness was a path open to all, beatifications and canonizations were very numerous. This option may have aroused real enthusiasm and brought great figures to the fore. For my part, today I plead for wisdom and prudence. It is necessary to open causes for beatification while witnesses are still present, but we should at least give ourselves the minimum time to carry out a serious long-term investigation, some fifty years after the death of the person concerned, for example. We risk blinding ourselves to personalities who are only discovered decades later to have been dangerous, even perverse and predatory. These decades are the time needed for possible victims to speak out. Refusing to rush is an ethical and spiritual obligation.

The most difficult question is that of the future of institutions whose founder was perverse and/or manipulative. Examples include Marie-Dominique Philippe and Marcial Maciel Degollado, founder of the Legionaries of Christ. Can these institutes be transformed when they took root in perversion, deviation, and fraud? There is no simple answer to this question. But at the very least, we need to be more vigilant and rigorous, with evaluation deadlines to see what is possible and what is not. The fact that some members have experienced great things does not in itself justify the preservation of a group. If even one thing remains unacceptable, then it is not possible to continue as it is.

We need to distinguish between what can be reformed over time, according to precise and clearly established procedures based on sound foundations, and what cannot. Our Protestant brothers and sisters do not have a monopoly on the term *reform*. The Church and religious orders have been able to reform themselves many times over the course of their histories, verifying the motto *Ecclesia semper reformanda*. And it is not just a question of "counter-reformation" or negative reactions to the prevailing mentality or the spirit of the time. It is about the ability to adjust to the Gospel in the light of social and human realities and the ever-renewed interpretation of the scriptures.

Finally, we must be careful when we invoke the parable in Matthew's Gospel that speaks of "good fruit" and "bad fruit," on the pretext that the community in question has many vocations, brings together many young people, celebrates fervent services, or produces acts of charity. A working group set up by CORREF invited us to reread this passage, which I quote here:

> Beware of false prophets, who come to you in sheep's clothing but inwardly are ravenous wolves. You will know them by their fruits. Are grapes gathered from thorns, or figs from thistles? In the same way, every good tree bears good fruit, but the bad tree bears bad fruit. A good tree cannot bear bad fruit, nor can a bad tree bear good fruit. Every tree that does not bear good fruit is cut down and thrown into the fire. Thus you will know them by their fruits. (Matt 7:15–20)

First, the Gospel invites us to distinguish between true and false prophets, shepherds and predators. When we speak of "good fruits," is it only in numerical or quantitative terms? There is real discernment to be made here. As the Dominican biblical scholar Philippe Lefebvre[3] has pointed out, for a tree or a work to bear fruit, it must be grafted onto Christ, in a life that is totally given to the service of the most vulnerable. In the words of the working group itself: "The model of biblical fruit-bearing is Christ. He is the fruit, and bearing fruit necessarily involves being configured to Him."[4]

3

THE PITFALLS OF FEMININE SPECIFICITY

Reintegrating Women into an Inclusive Church

Anne-Marie Pelletier

Let's face it: never has the Catholic magisterium declared such concern for women as during the three previous pontificates. Their promotion in society was a "sign of the times," as John XXIII had proclaimed. Shortly afterward, the last session of the Second Vatican Council paid them an unprecedented tribute. A breach had been opened. Women were promoted to the rank of Doctors of the Church beginning in 1970, a first in the two-thousand-year history of Christianity. Many variations appeared on "the dignity of women," to which John Paul II attached a cascade of laudatory qualifications. There was also, for example, the daring appearance in 2012 of a publication associated with the very official *L'Osservatore Romano* under the responsibility of a team of women called *Donne Chiesa Mondo*. Lastly, the election of Pope Francis gave rise to a real wave of confidence among many women, confronted with a pope who presented himself from the outset as the defender of a "women's right" that he said was still far too ignored, and which he had advanced in the Vatican by allowing some women to enter the bastion of the curia.

And yet the "women's question," as it is called, is still at the top of the list of urgent issues declared by Catholics around the world who took part in the major consultation in preparation for the synod in autumn 2023. It's a paradox that must not be sidestepped and must even be highlighted. Thus, in addition to the existential uneasiness of Christian women at work who are weary of their ever-subordinate status, how can we understand, for example, that it took almost fifty years to allow women only in 2021 to access the ministries of the lectorate and the acolyte, which were opened to men in 1972?[1] Why does the female diaconate still remain problematic, even though it has been the subject of much questioning and work that has in no way disqualified it in principle and that even legitimizes it in a version to be defined in line with the Church's present situation?[2] Why, more generally, at the time of the Synod on Amazonia, did the voice of Amazonian women, with their demands directly inspired by the field experience of the communities, ultimately find such a limited echo?[3] Why, again and again, this suspicion that any request from women would be a quest for power, when the men of the Church have remained untouched by this reproach? Or, to put it another way, why does the Sunday liturgy at Easter time ignore the account of the apparition to Mary Magdalene, which so explicitly charges her with announcing the resurrection? All this should end up disturbing us a little more. Finally, what are these brakes that are so powerful that they immobilize the Catholic Church, preventing it from overcoming its reflexes of restriction and from escaping endless procrastination, as soon as it comes to problems affecting women?

It's not enough to make "clericalism" the explanation. Too easily invoked, the word prevents us from analyzing the depth of the problem. In this case, we need to take a close look at the way in which even where the magisterium claims to be favorable to women, a rhetoric comes into play that is, in fact, a theology whose logic and effects are too rarely questioned. Today, we must dare to identify the way in which this theology, draped in lofty spiritual justifications, ultimately amounts to protecting an ecclesial order with its structure of discriminatory hierarchy and, above all, with the male exclusivism that characterizes the head of the Catholic Church. From this point of view, the question of the "specific feminine" can be a good point of observation, providing decisive lessons.

WHEN THE SPECIFIC IS THE STARTING POINT

Specificity is one of the leitmotifs of official discourses when they express themselves on women in the Church and question their access to new responsibilities; everything must be thought out, they warn, to respect the specificity of women, not to do violence to the specificity of their nature. Let's not masculinize women! they say repeatedly.[4] It's an old theme, in fact, that women's nature sets them apart and separates them from men. Note that this type of specificity has no counterpart; no one questions what the specificity of the masculine might be. The assertion of a feminine nature is a traditional argument. Men draw up the typical portrait from the reservoir of misogyny in society, and women must then model it. We shouldn't be surprised by this scenario since the masculine is widely believed to be capable of both expressing himself and embodying the universal figure of the human being. So, the masculine speaks for all men and women, justifying the fact that women remain silent and take what is said about them as being the truth of who they are.

In contrast to the potentially universal masculine, the feminine remains engulfed in a particularity that, whether consciously or not, constitutes a more limited version of the human condition. Whereas men are endowed with mastery, rational discernment, and all that makes them the natural and legitimate holders of authority, or even qualified stewards of the powers of the sacred, the feminine is stubbornly associated with the sphere of sensation, sensitivity, emotion, and instability. In a more laudatory version, we speak of intuition, receptivity, and interiority, qualities that are regularly invoked and that end up converging on the reference to maternity, that indisputable attribute that tends to be identified with the whole of the status of woman. The magisterium readily proclaimed that "the Woman is the Mother," with no regard for the complexity of women's experience of childbirth, with its sometimes tragic realities and, more than once, its subjection to male domination. The effervescent imagination of certain theologians who exalt motherhood goes so far as to elevate it to the level of the priesthood, explaining that, because a woman is a mother, she cannot be a priest.

One of the most powerful stereotypes makes the home the proper place for women, in contrast to the outside world, which falls under the jurisdiction of men and is open to their initiative, creativity, and enterprise. Authoritarian political powers, including those brandishing the "defense of Christian culture," continue today to advocate this model, which was obviously that of the ancient biblical world. In this respect, it is worth noting that the first chapter of the apostolic exhortation *Amoris Laetitia* (8) opens with a reference to a psalm that celebrates the family, but in which the psalmist only addresses a man: "You shall eat the fruit of the labor of your hands." The woman is evoked obliquely, related to the man, and existing only through her fruitfulness: "Your wife will be like a fruitful vine within your house" (Ps 128:2–3). The emphasis on this scriptural reference is likely to create some trouble by suggesting that this representation of the sexes continues to inhabit the imagination of the Church's discourse as an ideal. By the same token, it inevitably inspires the Church to defend the essence of the feminine, meaning the primordial, creative, and destinal identity that places at the threshold of every woman's life a model to accomplish, a program to fulfill that, in this case, is concentrated in the service of others, namely, care. This service is said to be the woman's affair, forgetting that it is just as much the man's concern, as attested in the Gospel story by the person of Jesus, whose life is entirely attentive to the flesh of others in all their states of call or distress.

Nothing is more tenacious than prejudice in this matter. A recent historian's account of women's laborious access to the pastorate in Protestantism during the twentieth century unfolds the history of men's resistance to the promotion of women and demonstrates that in the religious world, whether Protestant or Catholic, the same objections, whether expressed or tacit, serve to keep women at a distance from the stewardship of the sacred: women's nature makes them unsuitable for command and public responsibility, and their role as mothers makes them incompatible with the exercise of a pastoral role, the nature of which would be violated if it were shared.[5]

Finally, another stereotype feeds the "exception" of the feminine, the effect of which should not be underestimated, even today, in the management of the place of women within the ecclesial institution. We're talking about the age-old idea that women are dangerous and perilous for men, because they are seducers, temptresses, and, it seems, devourers of their virility. In the biblical tradition, it is Eve, of course, who forever embodies this in the subconscious, giving rise there as elsewhere to the same defensive reaction, namely, the supervision and control of women, especially exercised over their bodies and their speech. This control is recalled in the New Testament in a few words that are nevertheless highly effective despite their marginality, when the injunction "Wives, be subject to your husbands" (Eph 5:22) combines its effects with that of the letter to the Corinthians: "Women should be silent in the churches" (1 Cor 14:34) and with the words of the first letter to Timothy: "I permit no woman to teach or to have authority over a man." This last statement invokes the scripturally problematic argument that it was Adam who was formed first and that it was the woman, not he, who was guilty of transgression (1 Tim 2:12–14).

Under these conditions, it is difficult to avoid suspecting that the discourse of the feminine specific has something to do with the concern to protect the status of those who are sacramentally in charge of the governance of the ecclesial body. This specificity plays the role of a defensive principle: that everyone occupies their place, and that women do not encroach on that of men, in this case on the perimeter of sacred power and authority. In other words, behind the fear expressed that women will betray their nature by taking on functions that are today reserved for men, there are other fears that are not expressed but that explain the luxury of precautions deployed to keep them at a distance from the priesthood, even to the point of refusing them an ordained diaconate, although this ministry is now detached from the traditional priestly curriculum.

In the same vein, we must resolutely view as problematic a theology that is much in demand today, which thinks of the Church in terms of two principles that would constitute its identity, namely, the Marian and the Petrine. Thus, Hans Urs von Balthasar, one of the most important theologians of the twentieth century, associates the feminine, under the reference to the Marian, with the mystical identity of the Church. The woman, of whom the Virgin Mary is the jewel, would be the specific bearer and witness of this identity. Her specific vocation would be to embody the face of the Church as spouse, the highest qualification of the Church. On the other hand, the Petrine principle is assimilated to ecclesiastical power, the depositary of the authority to teach, sanctify, and govern the ecclesial body.[6] In this division, the Marian pole is given such prominence that it leads to the assertion that "women have something else, and much more." This is a superlative formula, but in reality, it is nothing more than a renewed version of the feminine specific, and a perilous one. The trap is obvious. It places the woman in an ideal sphere, so ideal that she does not have to commit herself by incarnating herself in the management of the institution's present. The fact remains that while the feminine thus acquires a supereminent qualification (women are said to be more spontaneously connected to God and the invisible, and therefore more apt to serve as the mystical face of the Church), it is indeed the masculine who still has the advantage of holding authority over all.

Nor does anything change by invoking the complementary nature of the sexes, another omnipresent argument. This does not upset the fundamental asymmetry in a Church where the presidency of communities and decision-making remain masculine, while women only ever provide the counterpoint of an auxiliary role to the clerics' mission. Not to mention that the Petrine believes and lives adorned with the unsurpassable prestige of having the function of representing Christ, whose person was that of a man, and whom only a man would be capable of representing. This is a highly problematic deduction in view of the most ancient theology of the incarnation, which in no way calls for the masculinity of Jesus but for his participation in humanity. So, the proclamation of faith is not that Jesus became man, in the sense of the word that contrasts him with woman, but that he became human (*anthropos*), that he was recognized as such (Phil 2:7), and that this is the pivot of salvation. A spirituality of the priesthood that ignores this reality will be inclined to make the priesthood an enclosure of sacredness—and of male sacredness—that must be doubly protected from women, but also, more generally, from the "laity," that subcategory of Christians, according to the hierarchy crudely expressed in the medieval formula, "There are two kinds of Christians, clerics and laypeople."

As long as this understanding of the Church remains the dominant reference point, we cannot hope that the Church will be truly renewed in the direction of greater evangelical equality. This is what leads us to believe that women's claim to the ministerial priesthood in an unchanged ecclesiology is not the right response. And, in any case, if the institutional order that is causing problems today finds one of its major supports in the discourse of the specific, this means that the real urgency is to rethink the Church, to restore it to its inclusive truth of Church-communion, making it possible for a new understanding and management of ministries to emerge. That is to say, the urgency is for the Church to make itself anew and generously welcome the "Christian novelty" it proclaims.

WHEN CHRISTIAN NOVELTY IS THE STARTING POINT

The newness of the Gospel is most forcefully expressed in the Pauline corpus. And, in a remarkable way, it affects particularly the relationship between men and women. It gives us a new, completely original version that masterfully challenges the misogyny of the few verses that have been trotted out over and over again and that stick in our memory. A passage from the letter to the Galatians, in controversy with correspondents fixed on the exclusivism of Israel, proclaims loud and clear the transformation brought about by baptism: "As many of you as were baptized into Christ have clothed yourselves with Christ." From then on, "there is no longer Jew or Greek, there is no longer slave or free," and "there is no longer male and female" (Gal 3:27–28). Three kinds of discrimination are therefore overcome, but the third is formulated a little differently from the previous ones. This suggests that it has been added here to a preexisting formula, which is also found in other letters of Paul. The words used are also surprising. They are not the ordinary designation of "man" and "woman" but take up the vocabulary of the first creation account in Genesis, when the first mention of humanity is immediately accompanied by its differentiation into "masculine" and "feminine," "male" and "female." In other words, the newness proclaimed by the Gospel relates to the original realities and, in particular, to what is at stake in the difference between the sexes, against the backdrop of the unity of humanity that Genesis begins to describe, and which is to be manifested at the end of the history that Christ inaugurates, with the overcoming of unequal differences.[7] This term, which has already been called to fulfillment, is the rediscovered access to the whole, in particular the reintegration of women into this whole, in which are found all those who, having been "clothed with Christ," are constituted "priest, prophet and king," as *Lumen Gentium* develops (34–36).

From that point on, everything changes and is transformed. The world of the Gospel comes into being, with women who manifestly accede to the condition of disciple, in fact if not yet in title. Some of them, freed from their domestic ties, go so far as to follow Jesus, the itinerant rabbi, on his path. Despite their legal status as minors, women are promoted to witness the resurrection, Mary Magdalene being given this role by Jesus himself. A whole world of stereotypes is shattered. Women are celebrated less for being mothers than for being believers; the impurity associated with the feminine does not exist for Jesus; the husband's will is no longer the only law in divorce; prostitutes, those women enslaved to men's libido, are snatched from contempt, and so on.

This newness permeates the apostolic Church. It is that of the Pauline Church, evoked in the first letter to the Corinthians, which teaches us to understand the Christian community as a body, an organic reality made up of diverse members linked by relationships of solidarity, since, Paul insists, all have been "baptized into one body...and made to drink of one Spirit" (1 Cor 12:13). It is still the Church, as it is taught to the Ephesians, who are exhorted to unity in vibrant terms, for "there is one body and one Spirit, just as you were called to the one hope of your calling" (Eph 4:4). And to serve this body, to provide it with the means for its vitality and mission, "charisms" are distributed that are clearly not reserved for men. This is demonstrated by the homage Paul pays at the end of his letter to the Romans, where many women are hailed with titles that prove their eminent positions in the mission and the exercise of responsibilities. At the head of the list is Phoebe, named *diakonos* in the Church of Cenchrea, whom Paul consecrates as his "benefactor" (Romans 16:1), followed by Prisca, Mary, Persis, and Julie. This Church is not a Church of men. It is a community (*adelphotes*), as it calls itself. And the texts suggest that, in a society based on the inequality of the sexes, this promotion of the feminine among Christians is bound to have caused problems. This certainly explains the alterations made in the later texts of the New Testament, when some of the strong prejudices of misogyny reappeared, reassuring the guardians of the established order.

In any case, this baptismal community is the foundation on which the Church began, and with this foundation we must now (re)begin. This is the conversion called for by the time of crisis we are living through. And this conversion implies that we approach the "women's question" by replacing the obsessive specificity of women with the primary reality of "all together," and by drawing the consequences in terms of everyone's identities, everyone's access to a voice, and the structures of governance. We also know how much experience on the ground supports this perspective today. The Synod on Amazonia, in particular, testified to the fact that diaconal responsibility was already clearly assumed by women, where women presided over the life of communities, ensuring the vital link with scripture, the transmission of the faith, and a basis for sacramental life, in places that were only occasionally visited by a priest. In Europe, the experience of Christian women in hospital or prison chaplaincies also suggests that there might be real relevance in delegating sacramental faculties, such as in the sacrament of the sick or the sacrament of reconciliation. Would this be such a daring innovation? Ignatius of Loyola received the sacrament of penance on the battlefield from one of his comrades-in-arms who was not a priest.

Obviously, we can see here that fears and defenses are making a strong comeback, even if it's not a question of cancelling the structures of authority in the Church but of restoring them to themselves, to their evangelical truth, beyond the disfigurements, or simply confiscations, that are causing scandal today. It is not a question of denying that the Church has a vital need to be constantly brought back to its source, nor of ignoring that Christians have a vital need to be constantly refocused on the call of Christ that is at the heart of baptism and the ecclesial mission. Nor is there any question of weakening the fact that the sacramental life must constantly be signified as the true resource of the Christian condition. All things that, if forgotten, simply cause the Church to collapse. But it is not said that this must be done through a sacred power, founding a hierarchy that would make some prevail over others, that men always walk one step ahead of women as in the ordinary life of societies.

In any case, what is at stake is not just a functional reorganization of the life of the Church or simply a redistribution of places and roles within an ecclesial institution that is globally unchanged. It is nothing less than giving substance to the reality proclaimed by Paul in the letter to the Galatians, of taking seriously this proclamation of shared baptismal identity and of embodying it, by moving it from a register of spiritual abstraction, which ultimately does not commit us to much, to lived life, to the architecture of the ecclesial institution, according to its double expression, masculine and feminine.

REDISCOVERING DIFFERENCE

For it is to difference that we must return in the end, not to polemically counter gender theories, as is often done in the Catholic world today, but because the entire biblical tradition argues powerfully in favor of the defense of difference as a condition of relationship and of life. In this case, a misunderstanding of the sentence in Galatians 3:28 would hear Paul cancel out the difference between the sexes. Rather, he is talking about establishing the difference in a new way, positively remade, in the strength of baptismal life, so that it is no longer parasitized by everything that makes it a vector of discrimination and inequality. This obviously implies, and this is a decisive point, that the recognition of difference must be preceded by the recognition of baptismal equality. In other words, it is a question of correctly ordering the common and the proper by ensuring the priority of the common. It becomes possible to rediscover the reality of difference in a healthy and positive way. In fact, we must not ignore that the Christian condition, like the human condition, is colored by different styles depending on whether it is experienced by women or men, even if there is obviously no question of a hermetical boundary. Women and men do not relate in exactly the same way to others, to life, to the flesh, to the test of time. In the same way, there are different ways of relating to God, of listening to God, of meeting God, of being in a verbal relationship with God. So, for example, if women have been so little involved in theological speculation throughout the history of Christianity, the reason is not only that theology was the preserve of men but that women were elsewhere. They were probably more inclined to encounter it in other ways, in other places, particularly where the encounter includes the trial of the night, because it is first and foremost an encounter of the heart, of love, as the Gospel story tells us, and which therefore exposes us to God in excess of words, reasons, and systems.[8]

In these conditions, too, we must remember that the Christian faith needs to be lived and expressed in a plural mode by combining the feminine and the masculine. The "God of all" cannot be the God of clerics alone any more than the God of men alone, or the God of women alone. Thus, God's face can only begin to take shape and be recognizable by associating the memory of Mary and Joseph bending together over the mystery of the nativity, of Simeon and the prophetess Anna united by the same expectation, the memory of the Roman centurion and the Canaanite woman together witnessing the expectation of the pagan world. There is also the memory of the double eagerness of the women and the apostles to go to the tomb, as well as the paschal encounters, that of Mary Magdalene in the early hours of Easter morning, and that of Peter in the other early hours, at the end of a fruitless night of fishing. The entire Gospel is a demonstration of Galatians 3:28, which finds its way into the cumbersome order of discrimination.

Let us conclude by emphasizing that Paul's declaration in Galatians 3:28, the reception of which has been postponed up to now, is not the utopia of a future or, in Christian language, the matter of the eschaton. It is the newness of the Gospel that wants to happen, to take concrete form *hic et nunc*, in the spiritual work to which Christians must commit themselves. The reception of this truth must be part of the program of this time, which is pressed by the experience of crisis and the need for resolute renewal. It is both an urgent need and a dynamic principle. When Pope Francis decided in April 2023 that seventy nonclerics would take part in the next synod on synodality, with equal voting rights—religious persons and laypeople, men and women—he was allowing the equality proclaimed by Paul to take shape a little better in the ecclesial institution. At the same time, he was simply bringing the working method of this synod into line with its purpose and the process of its preparation. This gesture constitutes a step forward that would not be right to ignore. May it enable us to have confidence in the future, confidence that will not be disappointed.

4

WOMEN IN THE CHURCH

From Guardianship to Empowerment

Marie-Jo Thiel

One of the most terrifying facts of modern life concerns sexual violence, spiritual abuse, and the abuse of power, especially against women and girls. Largely invisible in society and the Church,[1] these assaults, which sometimes last months and years, are crimes with tragic consequences for the victims. Feminism and movements such as #MeToo have helped to raise collective awareness, but many women are still under the sway of patriarchal, lordly, domineering, and macho figures, including in the Catholic Church. But societies have changed. Almost all the synod reports following the consultation of the people of God in preparation of the synodal assembly in October 2023 mention "women's issues" as a major area of "dysfunction in the Church," echoing the diagnosis of independent reports on sexual violence in the Church, such as that of CIASE[2] in France.

Women's voices denouncing gender discrimination and the de facto inequalities to which they have been subjected are now reaching the public sphere and the Church.[3] They bear witness to an emancipation that is underway and has become irreversible. Such emancipation has resulted in real empowerment through studies, professional work, ecclesial, social, and community commitments, and the like. *Gaudium et Spes* (8–9) already testified to this, but the challenge for the Church today has become more crucial: reform or die! Read the signs of the times and commit to ecclesial renewal, or risk becoming irrelevant and moribund.

The challenges are immense. The inclusion of women in the ministries of the Church has a strong symbolic value, given the incomprehensible nature of their exclusion. But the key to progress is the Church's willingness to break free from patriarchal patterns of thought and the systemic clerical "power-gender"[4] constellation that not only encourages abuses in the Church but also hinders the development of all God's people, women *and men*.

This essay will begin by observing and listening to women who draw from their Christian freedom to free themselves from domineering tutelage and to assume their baptismal responsibilities. It will then look at the "women's question" as a sign of the times in the synodal bodies. It will conclude with a possible *kairos*.

THE NEW VISIBILITY OF COMMITTED BELIEVERS

If the face of the Church during the COVID-19 pandemic was essentially that of priests celebrating Mass in liturgical vestments without a congregation[5]—an astonishing vignette of the institution reduced to figures of the sacred—a different picture emerges when we look closely at religious practice in today's parishes. What we see are the faces and voices of women emerging, not by choice but because of the disappearance of men. Taking part in Sunday Mass, teaching catechism, welcoming parishioners, animating groups of children…all these activities are being carried out almost exclusively by women. Admittedly, many women have also tiptoed off the Church ship, but fewer than men, at least until now. Perhaps women, scarred by secular coercion, are still trying to give the impossible a chance, a bit like the women who were the first to go to the tomb on Easter morning. The other disciples had fled, fearing the same fate as their Master, or because they had been disbanded. But the women who had witnessed the passion and crucifixion went to the tomb and became the first apostles, plenipotentiaries, "attorneys-in-fact,"[6] messengers of the resurrection. "During the first two centuries," recalls the Jesuit biblical scholar Jean-Bernard Livio, "Mary of Magdala enjoyed extraordinary prestige in the Christian communities. They even went so far as to call her 'the Apostle of the Apostles.' In some liturgies, she is named before Peter, because Peter denied her."[7]

Strengthened by the biblical renewal, many women are being trained, often more of them than men. They want to be of service to the proclamation of the Gospel and find in the scriptures a source of assurance and vitality. They are encouraged by social movements that are fighting for the emancipation and equality of women, not only in word but in practice, through the laws on parity, for example, or the reflections of anthropologists such as Françoise Héritier, who explains the cultural roots of the universal belittling of women and the appropriation (by men) of their procreative capacity, which is "extraordinary to produce bodies different from themselves." But, adds the author, "inequality is not an effect of nature....This symbolization is the foundation of the social order and the mental divisions that are still present, even in the most developed Western societies." However, this "very archaic vision" is not "unalterable"![8] Elucidating its mechanisms permits us to deconstruct it.

In this way, women are taking their history into their own hands. Christian women are discovering the extraordinary freedom Jesus had with women, in contrast to the prejudices of his time. They spot the baptismal equality that guided the "first" Paul but that was progressively buried despite the name *adelphotes* (unknown at the time) as the proper name of the

Church to express the vital link uniting the baptized man and woman to Christ the brother: "the baptized person receives 'fraternity' with Christ, with whom he becomes the 'coheir.'"[9] Unfortunately, cultural, historical, political, and social contexts gradually took over when it came to developing the ecclesial structure. The status and role of women were constrained by dogmatics, ecclesiology, pastoral care, ethics, and the like, as numerous recent studies have shown.[10]

This new understanding must now lead to urgent changes because discrimination and injustice are still experienced by women empowered by their active commitment in the Church. In addition, this desire is expressed by more and more Church leaders, including Pope Francis and the people of God who expressed themselves in the synodal consultations (2023–2024). While Vatican II marked a threshold, little has been achieved to date, and many believers have had the impression of growing resistance, if not retreat, since John Paul II's apostolic letter *Ordinatio Sacerdotalis* (1994), which declared that women could not be ordained to the Roman Catholic priesthood and that the Church had no authority to do so. Despite magisterial attempts to declare it "infallible," this text has not been accepted by the *sensus fidei*. But far from silencing women, and even more so the people of God, the interpretation of the signs of the times has led many believers to become even more committed to equality, strengthened by the Gospel of Christ and the Holy Spirit, who continues to call not only men but also women to the priesthood to serve the people of God.

Let us be clear, however, that this is not a question of allowing women to be integrated into a clericalist system, but the need to take into account the evangelical and baptismal passion for the equality of men and women, and consequently of seeking together, in a synodal way, new models of ministry accessible to all in a renewed Church. As Mary E. Hunt points out, "The chimerical idea that a Petrine principle and a Marian principle determine such questions is hypocrisy, not theology."[11] In addition, the "administrative route" to becoming a secretary or manager, advocated by Pope Francis, would be even more of a belittlement.

There must be genuine synodal co-construction, for, as *Gaudium et Spes* states,

> the Church has always had the duty of scrutinizing the signs of the times and of interpreting them in the light of the Gospel. Thus, in language intelligible to each generation, she can respond to the perennial questions which men ask about this present life and the life to come, and about the relationship of the one to the other. We must therefore recognize and understand the world in which we live, its explanations, its longings, and its often-dramatic characteristics. (4)

INTERPRETING THE SIGNS OF THE TIMES

Among the signs noted by John XXIII in his 1963 encyclical *Pacem in Terris* are "the entry of women into political life" and the fact that "women are gaining an increasing awareness of their natural dignity" and are no longer "allowing themselves to be regarded as a kind of instrument" (41). Sixty years later, the challenge of interpreting the signs of the times has become even more acute in a rapidly changing world, which has tragically intensified the warning signs both for women and for the Church herself.

What is at stake is not only the interpretation but also the implementation of the resulting changes. John XXIII speaks of the "signs of the times" because he is certain of the "consoling presence" of Christ (Matt 28:20), "especially in the most serious periods of humanity." Christoph Theobald echoes him, saying that it is "in such circumstances that we must understand his exhortation to interpret the 'signs of the times'...in an attitude of 'vigilance,' totally opposed to the 'discouragement' of those 'who see only darkness completely enveloping our world.'" John

XXIII was not naïve. In faith, "in the midst of this thick darkness, he discerns many signs that seem to herald better times for the Church and for humanity" because he "trusts" in the presence of Christ, who enables him to discern that "humanity is at the turning point of a new era."[12]

But if the time is right for recognizing the equal dignity of the baptized, why is it taking so long to make and take *practical decisions*? Why so much resistance? There are at least four key issues for the future of women and hence for the Church:

- Violence and injustice against women: an argument in the form of a cry
- The affront to the equal baptismal dignity of men and women: a recurring argument based on an analysis of practices
- Women's representation of Christ: a decisive argument from theology and the humanities
- God's call against all odds: a stimulating spiritual argument.

Violence and Injustice against Women

The German synodal path is edifying;[13] it investigated various topics, including the question of women, seeking to respond to the facts pointed out by the MHG report[14] with the best theologians and making well-founded proposals. In its theological orientation text, it states: "The cry of the victims of sexual violence is truly a *sign of the times*. This cry draws attention to a terrible evil, namely decades of violence during which priests, religious and other collaborators have abused their spiritual and administrative power over children and young people, but also over adults and especially over women."[15] It also highlights other problematic aspects of ecclesial life that have been experienced as injustices against women. The document mentions "the question of power and the need for separation of powers; the viability of forms of priestly life; the need for equal access of both sexes to the services and ministries of the Church; the reception of current research in the Church's teaching on sexual morality. These too could prove to be *signs of the times*." And dealing with them could contribute to "a new era," in the words of John XXIII.

However, it is not a question of exalting women by sublimating their "feminine genius," or of dangling the Marian principle (which would be "greater"[16] than the Petrine one!), offering Mary, the virgin and mother, as the only model. Mary is a figure who applies to both men and women. But in the clericalist constellation, this model becomes a means of subjugating and demanding docility, all the more so as women remain identified *at the same time with Eve*, the seductress, the manipulator, the accomplice of male decision-makers (a strategy of inverse victim-perpetrator). Many victims denounce this idealized approach to the figure of Mary, this "new Eve" turned into the original Eve in the language of the predator. Yet these injustices are not only the cause of suffering, but they also lead to a cascade of other injustices, to the exclusion of women from the possibility of officially representing Christ through the sacraments, of proclaiming him in the Eucharist, which many Christians, but also priests and bishops, find incomprehensible, deeply discriminatory, and incompatible with the Gospel message. "*We are outraged by the inequality between women and men, from the earliest age, within the Church.*"[17]

This growing awareness of the violence and injustice done to women and, through them, to the people of God (which also includes people with nongendered sexual identities) is and should be a sign of the times that calls upon theology as well as the human and social sciences. The future of the Church depends on it.

An Affront to the Equal Baptismal Dignity of Men and Women

The CIASE report, and its equivalents in other countries, is essentially in line with the feedback from synods in France and elsewhere. The French synodal document sums up what is at stake with point 2.3, "Men and Women: Living the Equal Dignity of Baptism": "If the service of women is valued, their voice seems to be ignored....At a time when equality between men and women has become commonplace, the way women are treated in the Church is not adjusted to their mission in her." Expressing so strongly the outrage against the equal dignity of baptism is in itself a "step forward," all the more so as it is supported by many other arguments.[18]

The major importance of the German text "Women in the Services and Ministries of the Church"[19] lies not only in the contributions to it by the best contemporary theologians but also in the experiences of the people of God with their bishops, and in a synthesis that seeks to be open to the universal Church. The document takes into account the tremendous progress made in Jewish and Christian exegesis (3). It also clarifies the social and cultural influence of the patriarchy and kyriarchy[20] on the writing, interpretation, and transmission of the scriptures and on the development of ministries and services. This makes it possible to distinguish the heart of the Christian faith from the cultural and systemic elements that have been added to it in various ways over the centuries. The Twelve, for example, are not to be confused with the "Apostles" (3.4, p. 25), who included women who witnessed the resurrection, received the outpouring of the Spirit on the day of Pentecost, and were described as "apostles, prophets and teachers" (1 Cor 12:28). This was an incredible innovation in the Gospel, given that at the time only men's testimony was legitimate in court. Paul detailed a beautiful collaboration between men and women, simple and natural, with no hierarchy based on sex. The document (3.5, p. 29) details this role of women in the New Testament communities, but also its reversal in the post-Pauline pastoral epistles, where women were once again excluded from the public community and relegated to the home (p. 30). A tribute to the kyriarchy!

The new ministries were soon reserved for men, even though "the office of deaconess is attested in the Western Church until the early Middle Ages....Women deacons were ordained in a manner similar to that of deacons" (p. 37 ff.). Not until the thirteenth century did Scholastic theology and canon law explicitly consider the exclusion of women from the sacramental ministry (p. 38) and their unsuitability for sacramental ordination, arguing that there was a "'natural resemblance' between the sacramental sign (implying the recipient) and the person designated by the sacrament. This means that the male Christ can only be represented by a male priest" (p. 38–39). The "justification of compulsory celibacy for clerics"[21] in the eleventh century also contributed to the "devaluation of women" (p. 39), priests' wives being branded "prostitutes and concubines, a source of sin and an occasion of perdition for clerics" (p. 39).

From the end of Scholasticism, mystical traditions challenged this ecclesiastical argument (p. 40), but these "testimonies remained invisible for centuries" (p. 41).

The German synod text also recalls the diaconate of women in the Orthodox Church (4.2) and the other Christian traditions[22] (4.3), which, unlike in Catholicism, led to the ordination of women at the end of the twentieth century. It calls for a broad and inclusive dialogue on the two magisterial letters *Ordinatio Sacerdotalis* and *Inter Insigniores* (48 ff.), which "do not adequately take into account the metaphorical nature of the texts" (Christ is masculine and the Church feminine), which "mystical traditions have always broken," and which cannot forget that "*in persona Christi* means the role and not the human person" in the modern sense.

Theological debates on women's access to the sacramental ministry must be set within the christological, soteriological, and eschatological perspective of the biblical texts and linked to the renewal brought about by Vatican II, which understands "revelation as a self-manifestation of God" (p. 53). They remind us that "Jesus Christ is the permanent image of the invisible God in time and history. God's nature is neither feminine nor masculine" (p. 51). Hence this almost quip-like conclusion:

> Anyone who, in this theological context, considers the undisputed biological sex of Jesus as a man to be important risks calling into question God's redemption

of woman, for only those who have accepted God in their human[23] nature are redeemed. (p. 53)

In a sign of the times, Vatican II took up the traditions of the early Church, based on the principle that there is a "multitude of *ministeria*" (p. 55) enabling the Church to carry out its central mission of evangelization. By relating the *in persona Christi* to the community of believers (p. 56), by designating the person who takes care of the poorest as representative of Christ (p. 56), and the like, this Council laid "the foundations for a renewal of the theology of ministries and sacraments" that "makes it possible to invalidate the argumentative figures of the magisterium with regard to the ordination of women" (p. 57). "The possibility of representing Christ in the dispensation of baptism is not linked to the male sex, so why should it be so in the presidency of the Eucharist?" (p. 58). And we are reminded of *Gaudium et Spes*, which calls for "the recognition of the fundamental equality of all human beings" and the elimination of "all forms of discrimination" (29).

Although it had to give up an explicit call for the opening of the priesthood to women in order to obtain a two-thirds majority of bishops, "an action text on women in sacramental ministry was adopted, with a strong vote in favor of the sacramental diaconate for women and the assumption of responsibility for promoting the debate on the opening of sacramental ministry to women, which must be conducted jointly by bishops and lay people."[24]

Women's Representation of Christ

Pope Francis was right to stress that the question of women's ministries cannot be one of "functionalization" or "clericalization."[25] Rather, it is about a renewed understanding of what the Church is and what ministries she needs, reflecting deeply on sacramentality and from an ecumenical perspective. The representation of Christ cannot be disconnected from an understanding of God's self-communication as a sacramental and soteriological event in which Christ's earthly masculinity plays no part. And this presupposes an effort at theological argumentation that has been lacking so far.

This is what two women professors of dogmatics have undertaken with a colloquium and a book bringing together the contributions of twenty eminent university professors of theology, in order to argue this central question of the representation of Christ when discussing the admission of women to the diaconal and presbyteral ministry.[26] It should be added that, in Germany, many qualified women are already serving and ministering at all levels of the Church and are able to administer baptism. In so doing, they are already fulfilling all the tasks of a diaconal ministry and are challenging the scientific and theological arguments on the *quaestio disputata* of Christ's representation. The scope of this question cannot simply be dealt with in an authoritarian manner; it must be critically questioned and answered in a way that is not an "intellectual sacrifice" (p. 14). The book proposes elements of sociological, philosophical, and theological reflection, then supports the biblical and historical-theological context, and finally analyses the ecclesiological and soteriological context. Once again, it highlights stereotypes linked to biblical and patristic traditions that the ecclesiological renewal following Vatican II must question in order to find new ways in which women are effectively witnesses to the resurrection, sent to proclaim the Gospel and thus stand in apostolic succession. Matthias Remenyi and Thomas Schärtl, for example, underline (p. 45) the role of the bipolar typology of the sexes in the current argument and consequently of the superimposition of the stereotypes of priesthood on those of masculinity, theologically overloaded with the biblical metaphor of the bride leading to ecclesiological exaltation. This image of the bride is certainly part of the rich inventory of ecclesial metaphor, but the authors point out that only since John Paul II has it had to carry the burden of the official theological justification supposed to legitimize the exclusion of women from the ordained ministry. Theological argumentation is all the more necessary as the representation of Christ is easily interpreted as a misunderstood "power."

Looking beyond this book, how can we fail to observe that the Christian churches that ordain women today are those that have (re)emphasized the reading of the Bible (*sola Scriptura*), at a time when Catholicism is concentrating on the Eucharist, and that are historically less linked to positions of power and wealth? The Catholic and Orthodox Churches are today becoming aware of the inequalities within them and of their harmful nature, but as Florent Guénard points out,[27] rational arguments are not enough to make egalitarianism a reality: what is needed is the passion for equality that gives a decisive impetus to reason. "We accept a lower rank if it is superior to other positions; we serve because we can command."[28] Now, the representation of Christ is first and foremost the work of all the people of God. As for evangelical passion, is it less powerful than a position of power?

God Continues to Call Women to Ordained Ministry

Theresa of Avila, Thérèse of Lisieux, Édith Stein, Madeleine Delbrêl,[29] and the like have all reflected on women's ordination. And we could add many more, because "for generations, many women have known that God has called them to the ministry of deacon or priest."[30]

Often, however, these women do not dare to speak openly about this calling, as they are usually immediately discredited and ridiculed with the phrase "are you looking for power?" And: "In the Church, we don't make claims...." Some are overcome by doubt or the scruples of not being able to respond to the Lord's call, and they decide to go on a retreat of discernment. But afterward, what should they do with a confirmation of this vocation? To analyze this reality, Philippa Rath sent an email invitation on April 26, 2020, to twelve women involved in the issue of gender equality in the Church. She was looking for testimonies from women who felt called to the diaconate or the priesthood and who had taken a step in this direction. Five weeks later (with a fixed deadline), she had received 150 responses from women, whose comments she recorded in a book. The first woman, for example, had felt called to the priesthood for a long time and asked herself about her life: "Have you finally followed your vocation or has a certain feeling of comfort or anxiety prevented you?" "What a waste of charisma and talent," the author finally exclaims![31]

Why is it so difficult for the male magisterium to hear these vocations? Why doesn't it take these existential encounters with God seriously? Isn't this going against the Spirit of God who persists in calling? Isn't this contrary to the wind of Pentecost that penetrates the interstices of all barricades? The Church must discern appropriately, using "criteria adapted to new circumstances, knowledge and experience."[32] It is not sex or gender, but competence in proclaiming the Gospel that should guide the allocation of ministries. "The signs of the times are a place of knowledge"[33] and "gender equality in the Church is an essential touchstone for the credible and effective proclamation of the Gospel to all people."[34]

LETTING WOMEN'S CHARISMS ENTER THE CHURCH

Numerous conceptual and cultural shifts have penetrated society and the Church. The emancipation of women has, for the most part, already taken place, but it still encounters limits and/or resistance, especially from those in power. Appointments of women to high positions in the Vatican are publicized by the magisterium as a matter of communication. They are welcome, but by not changing the status of women, they give the impression of being an instrument to maintain the clerical system, creating new injustices that are all the more painful because Christian women have moved from secular tutelage to evangelical empowerment and are more aware than ever of the obstacles and resistance.

However, the current crisis could become a *kairos* if it were accepted as a *sign of the times*, that is, as an urgent invitation to make and take decisions, as well as a *window of time* in which transformations are (still) possible where we can envisage new beginnings, including in the life of the Church. And isn't this *kairos* already underway in the various synodal processes, in the luminous collective elaborations of both the synodal path and the feedback of the synod of Bishops? The changes unveiled on April 26, 2023 (and put into practice in October) included the fact that seventy nonbishop members represented the faithful of the people of God with the right to vote on synodal decisions. The Holy Spirit continues to assist the disciples of the risen Lord by "rekindling the desire for synodality that the first Christian communities experienced."[35]

And what if today, as on Easter morning, women were messengers of the resurrection, called to be new apostles, plenipotentiaries for the proclamation of the Gospel, witnesses of the Living Life as much as men? Yesterday, they spoke to disciples frightened by the death of Jesus. Today, are they not speaking to Church leaders, some of whom are just as afraid of the changes that need to be made? Assuming their vulnerability, they witnessed the passion and drank from the blood and water that flowed from Christ's side. Strengthened by this, they returned to the tomb and were able to welcome the unexpected, the tremendous message of the resurrection, and proclaim it to the world.

Men and women are marked by differences, but never by the superiority of one over the other. Differences can be frightening and lead to power struggles, but this is not the way to build an authentic and constructive relationship. On the contrary, the relationship between men and women is an ongoing process of learning about otherness and coming to terms with it. The most difficult thing may be to listen to each other, to be attentive to the *sensus fidei/fidelium,* and to dialogue with the complex and discordant voices of "tradition" in the ecumenical sense and of the world in search of the respect for human rights. But in the end, whether we like it or not, "a culture of debate is well and truly taking root in French Catholicism, with which the episcopate must now reckon."[36] And because of the common priesthood, the people of God as a whole "cannot err in matters of belief" (*LG* 12).

But we have yet to embrace this *kairos* fully. The German orientation text of the Synodal Way for the Renewal of the Church sums it up admirably:

> The Spirit of God directs the believer inwardly towards that which determines everything and everyone.... In the sense of the faith of the believer, God's self-communication always occurs anew. In this spiritual event, believers assimilate the truth of Scripture, tradition or the signs of the times through inner conviction. (44)

What is more, as Gregory the Great said, by making the truth of scripture their own, believers make scripture itself progress![37] In so doing, they open up the future of the Church through the assumption of all the charisms of women and men in the service of the Gospel. Yves-Marie Blanchard summarizes in the form of a quatrain:

> No longer fathers but brothers, not just brothers but sisters.
> Not just the Twelve, but a variety of apostles, men and women, with no male-female competition.
> No longer great in the eyes of the world, but above all small, humble and poor of heart.
> No longer leaders with managerial ambitions, but simple pastors, close to and devoted to everyone.[38]

5

RENEWING THE CHURCH BY FOLLOWING THE SENSE OF THE FAITHFUL

Isabelle de La Garanderie

> Being Church means being God's people, in accordance with the great plan of his fatherly love.
>
> Pope Francis, *Evangelii Gaudium* 114

Speaking collectively about "Church Reform"? This is dangerous: would I dare risk it? This is the question I faced at the beginning of writing for this book; not only is the subject highly sensitive, as can be seen in discussions among Catholics, which quickly move toward verbal sparring when broached, but also because it involves writing alongside women who are different from me. Am I capable of engaging in this dialogue? Perhaps this is an opportunity to approach the subject with greater nuance and depth, even through the discord that may emerge!

The question asked here is the same one that is posed with acuteness and urgency to our Church, which has been blackened by so many scandals: Do we dare converse, even with those who do not think like us and who exist outside our ecclesial "bubble"? To do this, we must learn to listen to those who think differently. This may be one of the main challenges of "reforming the Church" at a time when we sometimes seem compelled to present a monolithic front to society, rather than allowing our diversity to shine through. However, for this we have tools within our magisterium, but we often forget them and, more critically, fail to implement them, despite Pope Francis's repeated calls for us to do so. What if "reforming the Church" means daring to rejuvenate it through all the lively and sometimes capricious streams it contains, different in their form, flow, or location, but all drawn from the same living water that flows from Christ's side?

DID YOU SAY "REFORM" THE CHURCH?

For Catholics, the word *reform* has historical connotations through its link with Protestantism since the sixteenth century, and it may seem synonymous with rupture. However, this word can also have a fully positive meaning, even within a Catholic context. In this, Pope Francis was of great help, a sign, perhaps, that we are in an especially favorable time to speak of "reform." Indeed, Pope Francis frequently used this term, including in significant moments such as his annual Christmas address to the Roman curia. This usage is particularly interesting because the pope was addressing those who formed, in a sense, his "inner circle," working to ensure the proper functioning of the universal Church through their mission around him in various domains. What he said here can be paradigmatic of a proper understanding of reform within the Church. While in 2014 he vigorously listed the diseases that could afflict the curia, by 2015 he proposed a way to overcome them, indicating that this applies to the Church as a whole with his statement: "we spoke of certain temptations or maladies—the *catalogue of curial diseases*; today instead I would like to speak about 'curial antibiotics'—which could affect any Christian, curia, community, congregation, parish or ecclesial movement. Diseases which call for prevention, vigilance, care and, sadly, in some cases, painful and prolonged interventions."[1] Thus, his words do not concern only his close collaborators but indeed all of us. He mentions the adage *Ecclesia semper reformanda*, that is, the Church must always be reformed, which has been brought back into focus within the Catholic Church particularly since Vatican II, as seen in *Lumen Gentium*: "The Church, embracing in its bosom sinners, at the same time holy and always in need of being purified, always follows the way of penance and renewal" (8).

Reform is not a question of lamenting about ourselves or weeping for our sins, but it is a vital and beneficial process because

> reform is first and foremost a sign of life, of a Church that advances on her pilgrim way, of a Church that is living and for this reason *semper reformanda*, in need of reform because it is alive. Here it must clearly be said that reform is not an end unto itself, but rather a process of growth and above all of *conversion*.[2]

Indeed, Pope Francis highlighted that the diseases and wounds of the ecclesial body—and we have since seen how real and numerous they can be—are, paradoxically, also opportune moments, "lessons and opportunities for growth, and never for discouragement. They are opportunities for *returning to the essentials*, which means being ever more conscious of ourselves, of God and our neighbors, of the *sensus Ecclesiae* and the *sensus fidei*,"[3] themes at the very heart of any reform of the Church. Francis also called for mercy to inspire every reform. In short, "ressourcement" or a "return to the essentials" thus appears to be synonymous with reforming the Church.

To better understand reform, we should consider the additional criteria given by Pope Francis, which he explicitly and extensively revisited in no fewer than six of his Christmas addresses to the Roman curia, clear evidence that this reflection held great significance for him and is one to which we must listen attentively. In 2016, Pope Francis framed the context of reform using a concept derived from Ignatian spirituality: *deformata reformare, reformata conformare, conformata confirmare et confirmata transformare*,[4] that is to say, "Reform what is deformed, conform what is reformed, confirm what is conformed, and transform what is confirmed." How should we understand this? This speaks to the very "form" that any reform in the Church must take:

> There can be no doubt that, for the Curia, the word *reform* is to be understood in two ways. First of all, it should make the Curia *con-form* "to the Good News which must be proclaimed joyously and courageously to all, especially to the poor, the least and the outcast." To make it *con-form* to the signs of our time and to all its human achievements, so as "better to meet the needs of the men and women whom we are called to serve."[5]

It is therefore not so much a question of inventing something new when we speak of reform as it is about restoring the Church to its true form, which is inextricably linked to the Good News of salvation in Jesus Christ. He never distanced himself from his contemporaries but always cared for them, drawing close to their cries and their misery. The Church, therefore, always transcends our temporal reality, but at the same time, it can only exist in the visible, the concrete, in the very soil of our contemporary world. Yet how many times, both individually and collectively as a Church, have we obscured Christ by turning away from our brothers and sisters? Moreover, instead of being rooted in the soil of real life, we sometimes walk along paths aimed at a disembodied ideal, forgetting that we are called to holiness in the very heart of our bodily reality. Thus, we are invited to abandon our "self-referentiality,"[6] our tendency to turn inward, and instead, to listen because "humanity calls and challenges us; in a word, it summons us to go forth and not fear change."[7]

Finally, it would be a mistake to hastily interpret this as a mere "horizontal" call to charity, as some criticize, implying a neglect of our relationship with the Lord. On the contrary, in all his addresses, Pope Francis never separated the Church's necessary reform from a process of conversion, both individual and collective, rooted in prayer. He explains that "the true soul of the reform are the men and women who are part of it and make it possible. Indeed, personal conversion supports and reinforces communal conversion."[8] These two dimensions are the first of the twelve that Pope Francis presented in his 2019 address. While some dimensions are more closely related to the concrete work of the curia, we also see, for the whole Church, the importance of Christocentrism, with the missionary dimension that must be at the heart of this process,[9] as well as the focus on synodality, catholicity, and discernment. In summary, to successfully carry out reform, acting in isolation is not enough; rather, one must be in relationship, both with the Lord and with all those around us, truly manifesting the original sense of *catholic*, meaning "according to the whole."

SENSUS FIDEI: THE SENSE OF THE FAITHFUL

Entering a process of reform requires, first and foremost, a posture of attentive listening. That each individual must listen attentively is based on the conviction that every faithful person has something to say and share because they possess what is technically referred to as the *sensus fidei*, the "sense of faith." Pope Francis frequently discussed this in vivid metaphor, referring to it as the "sense" of the sheep, which instinctively know the best path to find the finest nourishment. Thus, from the very beginning of his pontificate, in his programmatic text *Evangelii Gaudium*, he emphasized the importance of attentive listening for all, including the pastors of the Church, affirming that the bishops "will have to walk after them, helping those who lag behind and—above all—allowing the flock to strike out on new paths" (31). There is therefore a strong call for trust among the people of God as a whole. But what is *sensus fidei* exactly?

Historically, this expression "is not found as such in either Scripture or the official teaching of the Church before Vatican II," but it "has solid scriptural support"[10] as traces of it can be found in the attitudes of many individuals recognizing Christ in unexpected ways. After the ascension, it is the gift of the Spirit that enables the continuation and actualization of this *sensus fidei*, not least through the apostles themselves at Pentecost. Indeed, they "began to speak in other languages, as the Spirit gave them ability" (Acts 2:4), which leads to a gathering of the crowd where "each one heard them speaking in the native language of each" (Acts 2:6). In the continuation of this reception of the Spirit of truth and unity, the Church of apostolic times did not hesitate to involve the entire assembly of disciples in important decisions, all while praying. Similarly, in the patristic era, the fathers widely consulted one another, believing that "the entire Church was a reliable point of reference for discerning the content of the apostolic Tradition."[11] The unity of faith within the Church and the consent of Christians to decisions thus became a reliable criterion, as they were guided by the "inner teacher" beloved in Augustinian thought. This is probably what led Vincent of Lérins to write: "We must be greatly attentive to hold fast to what has been believed everywhere, always, by all."[12] Far from hastily reading this as a desire for immobility, one can, on the contrary, see the importance of seeking unity and true catholicity; it is the same principle we can observe at work in the early centuries, where, at times, laypeople seemed to stand firmer than certain bishops in the face of heresies. Certainly, they were not automatically consulted everywhere, but this concern for the search for genuine consensus is undoubtedly a path to be rediscovered for today.

During the medieval period, one often distinguishes between the Church of the clerics and the Church of the laity, which seems destined for a more passive role. However, it continues to be promoted, in various forms, that the Church as a whole is infallible in its "belief."[13] In the nineteenth century, we even find a form of "practical application" of belief in the sense of the faith with the proclamation of the dogma of the Immaculate Conception, as this was defined after consulting the bishops, not only for their own opinions but also regarding the piety of the lay faithful in this matter. In the bull proclaiming the dogma, Pope Pius IX places this common agreement on the same level as other sources for defining the Immaculate Conception of the Virgin Mary. With the current synods of bishops consulting more widely, are we not seeking to generalize this type of virtuous practice, making it more effective?

In any case, the expression clearly appears in the magisterium from Vatican II. First, the constitution *Gaudium et Spes* mentions it by considering that the *sensus fidei* is one of the great helps for promoting the values of marriage and family in the new times (52). But *Lumen Gentium* especially explains its characteristics and importance:

> The holy people of God shares also in Christ's prophetic office; it spreads abroad a living witness to Him, especially by means of a life of faith and charity and by offering to God a sacrifice of praise, the tribute of lips which give praise to His name. The entire body of the faithful, anointed as they are by the Holy One, cannot err in matters of belief. They manifest this special property by means of the whole peoples' supernatural discernment in matters of faith when "from the Bishops down to the last of the lay faithful" they show universal agreement in matters of faith and morals. That discernment in matters of faith is aroused and sustained by the Spirit of truth. It is exercised under the guidance of the sacred teaching authority, in faithful and respectful obedience to which the people of God accepts that which is not just the word of men but truly the word of God. Through

> it, the people of God adheres unwaveringly to the faith given once and for all to the saints, penetrates it more deeply with right thinking, and applies it more fully in its life. (12)

This paragraph follows a development on the common baptismal priesthood. The "sense of faith" thus appears as a manifestation of the prophetic dimension of the people of God as a whole. This document also specifies various essential defining traits: the fact that the people of God as a whole are infallible *in credendo*, that is, "in believing," which is linked to the gift of faith; that the *sensus fidei* pertains to both the ordained hierarchy and the lay faithful in the search for a "universal consent"; that it is a gift of the Holy Spirit subject to the magisterium; and that it enables the full reception of the Word of God. The second paragraph of section 12 of *Lumen Gentium*, dedicated to charisms and particular gifts, and section 13 to "the universality or catholicity of the people of God," are deeply interconnected; it is indeed about listening to what the Spirit says to God's people, both personally and communally, in order to be led "into all truth," which also allows us to "know what is to come" (John 16:13). This confers a fundamentally essential role to the *sensus fidei* in the temporal actualization of faith in the world and in the life of the Church. This last point underscores its importance for today.

The same document goes even further and adds, regarding the *sensus fidei* of the laity, that it is given "so that the power of the Gospel might shine forth in their daily social and family life" (35). *Presbyterorum Ordinis*, the decree on the ministry and life of priests, highlights the dialogical aspect of the *sensus fidei* by enjoining priests to recognize the various competencies of the laity, to "be able to recognize the signs of the times" with them, and also to demonstrate this *sensus fidei* in discerning, because "priests should uncover with a sense of faith, acknowledge with joy and foster with diligence the various humble and exalted charisms of the laity."[14] The International Theological Commission, for its part, defined the *sensus fidei* in this way in 2014:

> On the one hand, the *sensus fidei* refers to the personal capacity of the believer, within the communion of the Church, to discern the truth of the faith. On the other hand, the *sensus fidei* refers to a communal and ecclesial reality: the instinct of faith of the Church itself, by which it recognizes its Lord and proclaims His word.[15]

Pope Francis fully embraced this conciliar dimension, but he did so with his personal touch, marked by the culture of encounter that he continually promoted; the faith of one believer always needs that of another to grow and flourish. In other words, faith is one and common but is enriched and "nourished by the diversity of the gifts of the Holy Spirit."[16] In addition, his understanding was also rooted in his Latin American experience, characterized by a great respect for the culture of different peoples and expressions of their popular piety. He was therefore attached to the *sensus fidei*. He shared with religious individuals:

> When I studied theology, when, like you, I reviewed the Denzinger and the treatises to demonstrate the theses, I was struck by a formulation from Christian tradition: the people of God are infallible *in credendo*, in believing. I derived my personal formula from this, which is not very precise but helps me greatly: "If you want to know what Mother Church believes, turn to the Magisterium because it has the responsibility to teach it infallibly, but if you want to know how the Church believes, turn to the faithful people." Thus: "The Magisterium will teach you who Mary is, but our faithful people will teach you how to love Mary."[17]

Pope Francis took up this point on various occasions, this idea that the people of God cannot be wrong when they believe. However, it is important to listen to this "instinct" of the people of God as a whole, which is not always so evident in our current ecclesial mode of functioning. In reality, understanding the *sensus fidei* and its essential dimension to better reflect faith in the Church allows us to see it as a true foundation of synodality, well beyond all the representations that may prevail.

THE *SENSUS FIDEI*: THE FOUNDATION OF SYNODALITY

At the conclusion of the third extraordinary general assembly of the synod of bishops in 2014, Pope Francis said:

> When the Church, in the variety of her charisms, expresses herself in communion, she cannot err: it is the beauty and the strength of the *sensus fidei*, of that supernatural sense of the faith which is bestowed by the Holy Spirit so that, together, we can all enter into the heart of the Gospel and learn to follow Jesus in our life. And this should never be seen as a source of confusion and discord.[18]

This is the very principle of synods, the etymology of which clearly reminds us that a synod is about walking together. Do we not feel a sense of distance from this when we see all the divisions within our Church? It can sometimes be quite difficult to walk on the same road, the Christ, together. Among the concrete applications of synods, the most striking example at present is the Synod on Synodality, subtitled "Communion, Participation, and Mission." This indeed relies on listening to the people of God, to their *sensus fidei*, which is then discerned together at various levels within the Church and will ultimately be voted on by the ministers responsible for the communion of the Church, the bishops.

Should we stop there in reforming the Church? I think not. In fact, this synod is not just a "moment" in the life of the Church lasting a few months; it aims primarily to initiate or reinvigorate a true style within our Church so that our way of proceeding and living as a Church becomes fully synodal, a journey lived together within a Church that is not merely an external institution but truly "us" in fullness.

The synod has sparked numerous criticisms as well as overflowing enthusiasm in Western countries. But was it truly understood? Some express fears of intraecclesial revolution, others desire to start everything from scratch, and some even want to impose what they believe to be the only correct expression of faith simply because it pleases them. Thus, the foundation of synodality seems to have been missed. On the contrary, understanding synodality as grounded in the *sensus fidei* allows us to enter into a process that is both ecclesial and conducive to renewal. This involves recognizing that I need the *sensus fidei* of others in the Church to express my faith more accurately; as Christians, we are never sufficient on our own! This is the challenge of experiencing synodality with justice: knowing how to listen to one another to discern the "right paths for his name's sake" (Ps 23:3) and not imposing one's own thoughts on others, but allowing oneself to be influenced, even slightly, by what the other reveals of God. In this respect, introducing plurality wherever possible at all levels of the Church seems essential. We must never think that being separate among ourselves will better express God than the Body of Christ gathered in its diversity. But to live this, we must become a true Church of listening and of the Word.

A CHURCH OF LISTENING AND THE WORD

The *sensus fidei* is a strong call to truly walk together. Beyond the necessary introduction of plurality in the different organs and movements of the Church, it is urgent to create places for meeting and dialogue within the Church, where we too often tend to gather only for the Eucharist and, too often, among like-minded people. Certainly this is good, but we receive the Eucharist, the Body of Christ, precisely to live as the body of Christ in the world. How do we live this dimension concretely? Everyone is important in the Church, and we must be keenly aware of this, urgently deepening our baptismal fraternity. Here, two dimensions need to be considered: those who express themselves and the manner of doing so.

If we take the *sensus fidei* seriously, we should remember that the most active among us may not be the ones to indicate the right path to take, but the path may be indicated by the most marginalized: the invisible, the broken, those battered by life, or even those who feel abandoned by the institution. This is certainly counterintuitive when we gather among people engaged in the Church to discuss this or that topic, yet it is truly the path of Christ who has always listened to the cry of the poorest. Moreover, it is concerning them that Pope Francis speaks again of the *sensus fidei* in *Evangelii Gaudium*:

> This is why I want a Church which is poor and for the poor. They have much to teach us. Not only do they share in the *sensus fidei*, but in their difficulties they know the suffering Christ. We need to let ourselves be evangelized by them…to embrace the mysterious wisdom which God wishes to share with us through them. (198)

The universal character of the instinct of each baptized person is reaffirmed here with force; even those who are too often the most neglected have the right to express themselves, and each person's duty is to listen to them. The poor are also particularly close to the suffering Christ, and that is why they have a significant role to play. This idea opens wide the door to a possible communion among all, rich and poor alike, that is called to be strengthened in a striking way during the Eucharist that brings us all together, with and for a renewed missionary impulse. Furthermore, it is not appropriate in this process to place clergy and laity in opposition but rather to envision them in synergy. All must be consulted, but two categories of people will play a particular role: theologians and the clergy. Theologians illuminate through reason what emerges from the synodal process and also help distinguish the realms of rationality and emotion, which are too often blurred today in our parishes. Members of the clergy have a specific role as the ministers responsible for the care of unity who must regulate and unify what they have received. This is not ex post facto censorship but rather a way of receiving these contributions to better discern how the Church as a whole should move forward, in accordance with Christ and the circumstances of the present time, in communion with the various local churches. This is a plan of action that should not be carried out alone, nor in isolation from what has been said.

The second dimension is the manner of doing things. In the Church, we too often adopt self-censorship, especially in front of authority. This creates silences, which we have seen can be deadly, preventing the *sensus fidei* from expressing itself and leading to a state of mere conformity. On the contrary, as Pope Francis invited us, we must develop the virtue of *parrhesia*, which etymologically means "to speak everything," that is, freedom of speech. A good explanation of this is provided in *Gaudete et Exsultate*, where it is stated that the source of *parrhesia* is Jesus saying, "Do not be afraid" (Mark 6:50) to the apostles and to us, encouraging us to walk and to serve with courage. Pope Francis says, "Boldness, enthusiasm, the freedom to speak out, apostolic fervour, all these are included in the word *parrhesia*. The Bible also uses this word to describe the freedom of a life open to God and to others" (*GE* 129). We need to find and promote freedom of expression: What are we afraid of? Thus, the preparatory document for the Synod on Synodality suggested the following words regarding the act of speaking: "Everyone is invited to speak with courage and *parrhesia*, which means combining freedom, truth, and charity. How do we foster a style of communication that is free and authentic within the community and its various organizations, without duplicity or opportunism?"[19] This is still the question addressed to us today; are we capable of promoting and welcoming free expression, or are we afraid? Some might indeed see this as a sign of a Church that risks going with the flow of society, but if we base our discourse on the primary listening of all to the word of God, what do we have to fear except refreshing our faith?

Rediscovering the meaning of listening to the *sensus fidei* is a major avenue for reform of the Church that resonates like a renewal. It challenges us to an act of faith that the other has something to tell us about Christ for us to believe together. Thus, by learning to listen to what emerges from each person, we move away from our self-referentiality and our comfortable certainties in order to hear what "the Spirit is saying to the churches" (Rev 2:7), to embrace the gentle and refreshing breeze that will emerge from it, and to carry the good news of Christ to our contemporaries.

6

BUILDING RELATIONSHIPS WITH THE VERY POOR

A Path to New Life

Laure Blanchon

Since the revelation of the multiple abuses, offenses, and crimes committed by Church officials and the highlighting of the systemic nature of the current crisis, many people oscillate between contradictory feelings: anger, despair, shame. It is impossible for many baptized people to imagine a future for the Church and, even more so, to imagine themselves a member of this Church in the future. Others lock themselves into a form of introverted assertion of their identity and into rigid practices to arm themselves against any criticism of the Church. From both perspectives, the ecclesial future seems closed. But in certain ecclesial places engaged in relationships with the poorest people, another type of experience has been unfolding in recent years, and a joyful vitality is emerging.

In May 2023, the Church in France commemorated ten years of "Diaconia 2013—célébrons la fraternité," an ecclesial journey proposed to all dioceses from 2011 to 2013, which culminated in a five-day gathering in Lourdes in May 2013.[1] Many groups that bring people in precarious situations together and in covenant with people who do not know this experience of deep poverty existed before this event and enabled this event to take place. But since then, a dynamic of diakonia has been launched in the dioceses of France, and many groups have emerged that share the word of God with people in precarious situations and that have permeated the local ecclesial fabric. Some of these groups, linked together in the Saint-Laurent Network, have been on pilgrimages to Lourdes and the Holy Land. Members bear witness to a new life within them thanks to these meetings, and it makes them missionaries in their everyday life situations. What is happening here? Where does this life, this joy, this impulse come from? Would building links with Christians living in great precariousness open up new hope for the Church? Can we imagine that the very poor would have a voice and a contribution that could renew the future of the Church?

In our human and Christian communities, poor people are often considered to be negligible contributors with nothing—or nothing interesting—to say, people who understand nothing and do not know how to do anything. However, those who spend time with them experience that this is false: people in precarious situations speak willingly when they are confident, and they often bring a new perspective on life, on God, and on the Church. But to understand this, we must leave behind our more or less conscious fears, our desire to keep these people at arm's length, which sometimes expresses itself in hostility and even contempt toward them. Then, we must overcome our resistance to welcoming them and listening to them. When they speak, we must be "waiting to hear"[2] an unheard voice, a word never heard before. We must be ready to let ourselves be surprised and moved by them. This requires struggle and an inner conversion on our part, but I am convinced that combining their contributions with those of other members of the community can give shape to a new and unexpected path in the Church.

Can we try to clarify how the very poor contribute to opening a future for our Christian communities?

BECOMING GOOD NEWS TOGETHER

In the current context, appearing publicly as Christians is not always easy, both because of resistance from society and the shame that we carry since the publication of the report by the Independent Commission on Sexual Abuse in the Church (CIASE).[3] This instills a tendency toward self-segregation and self-referentiality, with a real risk of communitarian withdrawal. Indeed, our assemblies often have little social difference, a great homogeneity of age and ecclesial sensitivities, and an unconscious culture of collusion and self-centeredness, lived in fear of the outside world and in search of mutual confirmation. All of this constitutes an obstacle to the credibility of the Church and its mission.

Therefore, Christian communities face the challenge of openness. To reconnect with an evangelical missionary impulse, it appears necessary to seek out and to savor encounter, to value otherness, to look outward and value the words of those who are different, and to enter into a culture of conversation and dialogue within the assembly of the people of God, in the joy of being together, welcoming new people and going out toward lesser-known social environments. The question then arises of discerning who these "lesser-known" people of our ecclesial environment are. We can be guided by looking at the path taken by Jesus Christ.

The pages of the Gospels are filled with people marked by great poverty, misery, illness, demoniac possession, social and religious marginalization, and death. They burst into the presence of the Nazarene to beg his assistance and to be lifted up by him.[4] Sometimes these poor people touch Christ through their faith or the gift of themselves, and they inspire him, like the Syrophoenician woman, the poor widow with her mite, the woman who was a sinner and who washed his feet.[5] Sometimes, like Bartimaeus, they become true followers of Christ. However, while they were at the heart of Christ's ministry, the very poor are often missing from our communities and little involved in the current synodal journey.[6] When they are present, they are perceived as beneficiaries of ecclesial charity and rarely positioned as actors and animators in the life of the Christian community. Our ecclesial life is atrophied by their nonparticipation, and the credibility of the proclamation of the Gospel is jeopardized by our attitude toward them.

This reveals a missionary emergency: In the name of our fidelity to Christ, how do we bring ourselves close to the very poor, look for ways to encounter them, put "the peripheries" at the "center of the Church's journey" (*EG* 198), and discern that it is there that we find the vital center of the Church?[7]

What can Church communities experience where baptized people choose to take this path and enter into long-term relationships with very poor people?

When some people decide to form lasting covenant relationships with people on the margins, multiple transformations take place in their relational manner and their priorities. Thanks to this long-term healing relationship, very gradually some of the poorest people dare to risk a relationship and approach the word; they then introduce into ecclesial relationships a radical otherness through their unique human and spiritual experience. Whoever listens attentively to them experiences the prophetic force of their word. They speak words never heard before about God, about Jesus, about life, about the mission of the Church; these "unheard" words move and amaze those who listen to them. Through their often direct comments on the relational wounds they have suffered, they reveal truth by unmasking the dynamics of exclusion and indifference that mark our assemblies; they call for conversion when they show how necessary they are as stakeholders in an ecclesial, social, and communal relational fabric.

Set in motion by this prophetic word of the poor and inspired by Jesus's friendship for the poor, members who are well integrated into the human and ecclesial community can choose to commit themselves to lasting ties with people wounded by misery. Through the bonds that are forged, these baptized people experience a gradual change in their priorities and are introduced to other ways of living together.

The first thing we notice is that the poor cause people to look at relationships differently. Whereas our ease of living can make us believe that it is possible to live by oneself and for oneself, independently of others, the lives of the poor, marked by being at the edge of radical vulnerability and by forms of death, demonstrate the impossibility of living without connection and in relational independence. The very poor do the work of truth. They return to what is elementary and show that human beings only live through benevolent and inviting human relationships. These links are life giving; they draw us from death and call us to life. Without caring relationships, human life is impossible.

Furthermore, in our social ties, including in the Church, we often think in terms of comparison, efficiency, results, and perfection, all terms that systematically disqualify and neglect the destitute, who end up being thrown away like waste, abandoned to indifference (*EG* 52–54). Those who want to live in communion with them witness the serious wounds that this thinking inflicts on the very poor, and they then seek to foster relationships inhabited more by esteem and respect for others, with the right to make mistakes and to try again, with the discovery of the inalienable dignity of each person even when their ideas and ways of doing things are unexpected and different. At the heart of these relational lessons of how to live together when we come from such different worlds, the very poor reveal the centrality of forgiveness given and received in order to endure in relationships.[8] Thus, Church cells that choose to engage in lasting relationships with the poor learn, step-by-step and through much trial and error, to move from positions of exclusion to a dynamic of caring hospitality.

Engaging in long-term relationships with the very poor also has a profound impact on our relationship to time. The very poor, so tested by life and so often humiliated by us, need a lot of time to dare to take the risk of trust, of relationship, to dare to express what they think and show what they create, and to dare to name their spiritual experience with Christ. Choosing to be in a respectful relationship with them means deciding to adjust to their rhythm and their needs. The diktat of "everything, right away" and immediate effectiveness must give way to the initiation of processes with a trusting consent to the delay that this implies. Furthermore, prioritizing their participation leads to encouraging more cooperative pedagogies and to an increase in conversations and collaboration. To participate, the very poor need conditions adapted to them and encouragement that builds confidence. They need support and patient interlocutors who take the time, like midwives, to allow them to access what they think. From then on, the poor can lead members of the Christian community on the path of patience, of reciprocity, and of joy in walking together, all receiving from one another.

Through these transformations that the very poor initiate among those baptized who choose to enter into lasting relationships with them, there is emerging incrementally a relational style that is more attentive to those who are last, a style ready to adjust to the rhythms and steps of the smallest, happy to be hospitable to those who are different. Each one is again brought into being by these new relationships, and little by little a sense of living together evangelically emerges. These changes, or conversions in relationships, experienced first in ecclesial groups, can affect other dimensions of people's lives and resonate in their interpersonal connections as well as in short- and long-term social relationships in which they share the little "music of the Gospel."[9] Through the links forged with the very poor, the heart of the ecclesial mission appears in a new light: it is mainly a question of humbly evangelizing the relationships between the members of the Christian community who become servants of the life of all and the life in all.

Church cells that dare to have a communal encounter with the very poor find themselves pulled outside of themselves. Their members gradually learn to welcome each other and to walk together. They start to live and to "propose a way of life with the taste of the Gospel" (*Fratelli Tutti* 1). A community in which respectful and lasting links exist between people from very diverse backgrounds can become good news proclaimed throughout the world. Perhaps some contemporaries will read it as a credible sign of the Gospel.

EXPERIENCING SALVATION TOGETHER

Being in relationship with very poor people who are familiar with experiences of public discredit, shame, and exclusion could open members of Christian communities to a different relationship with the experience of humiliation and despair in the face of a possible future for the Church after the revelation of the abuses and crimes committed by ecclesial leaders. These meetings could help some to reconnect with confidence in the vocation of the Church. How?

If instead of retreating into its hurt and shame, a Christian community allowed itself to be affected by the poor's experiences of humiliation and rejection, and if it opened itself to their call, deciding to become close to them, a life path could open up for both.

With their confidence built up and supported with kindness, people in precarious situations through the life-giving connections woven over time could experience a transition from death to life, a journey through radical adversity, and a reconnection with the possibility of living. However, others may be so injured that they never manage to emerge despite many attempts to raise themselves up, and they die prematurely without being able to grasp the hands extended toward them.[10]

Experience shows that it is also important to help people put into words the journey they have lived through. "For people who have been very tested by life, writing a life story is a path to liberation, recovery and coming to oneself." Very often, "it is not possible for them to discern meaning and coherence in their existence" as it is so chaotic, "and most have too few linguistic and conceptual tools at their disposal to do this interior work alone."[11] There is a real possibility that their lives remain "severed pieces," as explained by Marie-José Perdoux.[12]

Through a process of discernment while learning to review their life, people can begin to put into words and name their experiences of passing from death to life. Such projects for learning to write one's life story exist in several ecclesial groups in France and are an integral part of the pedagogy developed in diocesan diakonia and communities with people from the Fourth World.[13] During the project, "the person is accompanied in remembering the events of their life, reading sense into them, discerning a purpose for their existence, and reporting on them" publicly in the form of a story. These processes help the person "to put into words their humanity which is in the process of construction and to discern the meaning that carries their life forward."[14] From then on, they can better access their identity, discern their strengths and weaknesses, and identify the connections that are points of support for today and tomorrow. In doing so, the person becomes more proactive in living. A path out of shame and lack of esteem gradually emerges, leading to confidence in oneself and in life.

These life stories of the poor can become words of life for everyone. Indeed, if members of a community listen to these stories and give credence to the words addressed to them by these very poor people, then they are sent back to the power of life that the Church carries within herself without always being conscious of it. The Church is a disciple of the risen one, capable, like Peter and John, of raising the cripple at the Beautiful Gate of Jerusalem (Acts 3:1–25), bearer of a treasure of life that she is commissioned to share with the world, a messenger of the "Prince of life" (Acts 3:15) and, in him, sacrament of the salvation of all (*LG* 48).

In such a process of walking together over time, the baptized experience that the salvation of Christ is transmitted to Christian communities by the poor with an unprecedented force because they demonstrate salvation by their experience of being counted as nothing and having their existence radically threatened. At the heart of this, they manage to stand up in life and bear witness to it.[15] This experience of relationship with the very poor allows the community members to feel "the saving force of their existence" and raise awareness of the merits of putting them "at the center of the Church's journey" (*EG* 198).

Making space for the very poor in our ecclesial life, being in relationship with them and connected with them, listening to them with attention and interest, and letting ourselves be taught by them gradually leads some believers to revisit what characterizes salvation in the Christian tradition, thinking of it in a less individual way. They perceive it as happening not only at the end of earthly existence but in new and more existential harmonics.[16] As I have already mentioned, salvation shows itself in a relational story. Salvation happens in and through relationships; an ecclesial/social body and relational play between several people are needed. It unfolds in a story; it is on the way, and it has already begun. We can identify experiences of salvation, of life being stronger than death, but salvation remains precarious in the lives of people. At the same time, it calls for a full deployment and makes a promise. We can also see that salvation is not conditioned by release from the grip of misfortune. When it happens, it does not remove the misfortune/misery that continues to affect the person. The person's existence often remains very chaotic, and yet they affirm: "God saved me," or "I was saved." The experience of salvation thus manifests itself less through release from misery and unhappiness than through the opening in the person of a capacity to give credence to life and through the memory of an experience of the faithful presence of others—God or a human person—which reopens the path to life. Finally, we can note that salvation is a gracious initiative of God that is received and welcomed, "a gift from God," according to Charlotte, a woman supported by the Diaconia of the Diocese of Fréjus-Toulon who gave her testimony on the radio program *Parole de vie*.[17] Some receive this gift, but mysteriously others sink into death without having been freed.

Paying attention to these less usual overtones of salvation sharpens the perceptions of some in the community and allows them to develop a new ability to discern salvation at work in forms they had not previously been aware of. Although little acquainted with ecclesial dogmatic formulations, these community members become more sensitive to the experiential categories in which salvation resonates in the lives of the very poor. Thus, they are empowered to recognize salvation already at work and to announce it in renewed categories, perhaps more understandable for our contemporaries.

Members in the Christian community may recognize that the Lord works salvation in the lives of very poor people who get back on their feet through baptized people who bond with them. They can then only marvel at the gift of God and be astonished at the trust that God places in the baptized to be witnesses of the risen one. This happy experience of being, through communal bonds, awakeners of the life deposited in those who are mistreated by existence could help some to believe again in the life potential of the Gospel and to take a new look at a future for the Church.

RECEIVING GOD FROM THE VERY POOR

Lasting connections between members of the community, some living in great poverty and others without this experience, can open a path of new life to the Church.

Vatican II's constitution *Dei Verbum* explains divine revelation thus: "In his goodness and wisdom God chose to reveal Himself and to make known to us the hidden purpose of His will (see Eph. 1:9) by which through Christ, the Word made flesh, man might in the Holy Spirit have access to the Father and come to share in the divine nature" (2). Continuing the reflection, a few paragraphs later, the text specifies that "through divine revelation, God chose to show forth to manifest and communicate himself" (6).

But without the presence of the poor in our Christian communities, we risk misunderstanding who God is. The very poor, "familiar with suffering" (Isa 53:3), lead us to know God in the highways and byways (Luke 14:23). By listening to them witnessing to their encounter with God, we discover that God reveals Godself as faithful, becoming Emmanuel—God-with-us. Even in human misery and deep humiliation, God opens paths where nothing seemed possible.[18] Thus, the very poor, "in addition to participating in the *sensus fidei,* through their own sufferings know the suffering Christ" (*EG* 198). They exercise toward other members of the ecclesial community a mission of revealing Christ in his suffering, because they have this experience in their own lives.[19] "In the heart of the Church, they allow us to encounter Jesus, because they speak to us about him, not so much with words, but with their whole life."[20]

We still have a step to take. As Pope Francis stated in *Evangelii Gaudium*, the baptized are called to "welcome the mysterious wisdom that God wants to communicate to us through them" (198)—the poor—and even more, to experience that they "give us Jesus himself."[21] Thus, not only is God made known through the poor, but even more radically, God communicates God's very self through them.

However, it should be noted that the dynamic of God giving Godself through the poor can only be developed within a kindly and relational fabric and by words that are full of esteem, in which and through which the poor come to themselves and to all that they carry in their life. This journey of life, of liberation, of recovery, and of coming to oneself is done gradually according to the trust experienced in relationship with the Lord and with a person in the community, then again with another, then with another....As a result, the person experiences themselves no longer in disconnection and sinking into anonymity[22] but carried over time by a fabric of connections. Something new can then happen in them and around them.[23]

When, reinforced by such a fabric of connections, persons in great poverty take the risk of opening up to the grace received from others or from God and choose to respond to it, they are touched and drawn into the dynamic of self-giving that inhabits God.

The very poor freely put their person and their entire existence at stake. They "entrust themselves totally and freely to God" (*DV* 5) and to others; they offer themselves without reserve into the hands of the Father and of their brothers and sisters in humanity. Why? Because, aware of their radical poverty, they experience that their life is totally given to them by others and by God. In response, they also want to offer themselves totally and give themselves to others and to the Father. They enter into a dynamic of gratitude and overflowing grace; happy to have been filled with grace, lifted from the abyss, freed from constraints, and revived, they in turn want to fill others with grace, to help them rise from death and to become free from constraints, and to contribute to their vivification.[24] They commune with God and God's life and enter into an experience of self-communication. They receive God, and they receive others. They respond by giving themselves.

Thus, the very poor can be our teachers in our Christian communities, our initiators in learning to participate in the dynamic of divine life amid human life. In this sense, we can recognize that they carry out a diakonia of the mystery of God in the heart of Christian communities. The ministry they exercise opens unsuspected ways for the Church to commune with Christ and become a sacrament of divine life in the heart of this world.

Forging lasting links between people who experience extreme poverty and people without this experience opens unexpected and beneficial paths. These links make the Gospel take shape in the world and make tangible the promise of new life made by the risen one to his disciples.

7

ONE CHURCH CAN HIDE ANOTHER

Anne Soupa

Church reform is a subject as eternal as comments on the weather. *Semper reformanda*, they say. Moreover, in these years of shame following the abuse scandals, reform seems so urgent that we would like to have it started already. Time is running out, and all the undeniable signs of entropy are there: an enormous decline in practice and sacraments, disinterest and even distrust of the opinions from those in authority, wear and tear on language and the great myths of reference, and rigidity on the part of governing bodies. Given the scope of the areas for reform, I will focus on just two. These are inclusion and inculturation.

THE WAY OF INCLUSION

Inclusion is a priority. The Church must be the common home of all; the sacraments are not for the pure but for those who need them. Achieving this is not a dream but the central project of the Gospel. Jesus's absolute priority was the rejection of exclusion, whatever form it may have taken. Of course, who would not agree to fight against poverty, but it was Jesus who said to Judas: "You always have the poor with you" (John 12:8). And it was Jesus who authoritatively reintegrates all those who are on the margins of society. These include women, to whom he speaks without concern for protocol (the Samaritan woman), the sick who were considered impure (the lepers, the woman with bleeding), the forgiven sinner for whom much will be forgiven, the religious outliers (the Samaritan woman), tax collectors (Zacchaeus), and even the possessed (the man from Gerasa whom Jesus sends home "in his right mind" [Mark 5:15]). Jesus has a sense so compelling, so divine perhaps, of the greatness of the human community that it makes him radically refuse to omit a single person. He is the Good Shepherd who does not let even the smallest sheep go astray. To this end, he denounces and overrides all divisive undertakings.

However, very early in history, the inclusion practiced by Jesus proved difficult, if not impossible, to maintain. Beginning in the year 150, by breaking with Marcion, this Church born from an excluded person began to exclude. It is a tragedy from which no one can feel free, as it profoundly questions the demonic propensity that inhabits the world. Yes, exclusion is, strictly speaking, the work of the devil, the divider who separates and makes us jealous of others. For around fifty years, in a world that also divides and excludes, the Church has once again become the exclusion machine that it has long been. The list is long....

Without even mentioning the all-too-frequent use of marginalization that allows the Church to avoid conflicts, nor the support of certain movements piously labeled Catholic, there are many categories of people affected. Those who are divorced and remarried as well as sexually active homosexual people are excluded from the sacraments, and women are victims of a radical, ontological exclusion. If, through subtle provisions of the Synod on the Family[1] the reintegration of the divorced and remarried (at least of those who have not yet left) is taking place little by little, the integration of women is far from being not only effective but even discussed. Women's integration into the decisions of the Church was the first request of Catholics when they responded to the synodal questionnaire. The scandal, however, has been denounced for a long time by the voice of women intellectuals who had deconstructed the artifices by which their submission was perpetuated[2] and by the voice of numerous activists in North America, Germany, Switzerland, France, and through our two voices, that of Christine Pedotti's and mine.[3]

Catholic women, deprived of any participation in decisions because they are excluded from the priesthood, which, since the Gregorian Reform, has been the source of all power, remain eternal minors in their own Church. To get around the problem, the Church relies on the concept of equal dignity of all the baptized. In this way, she attempts to reconcile an egalitarian ontology and a differentialist capacity. This would justify differences in aptitude between men and women for certain responsibilities, such as the priesthood or the diaconate. But it has now been proven that granting responsibility to a few makes others invisible to the point of forgetting the "equal dignity" recognized by all. Furthermore, male privileges have become not only unacceptable but incomprehensible in today's society. How can we understand that the priesthood is the prerogative of one sex? Do they celebrate with their penises? If this were true, it would show great disrespect to the Eucharist!

How can we give women access to responsibilities equal to those of men? Two modalities are possible: priestly ordination or the promotion of baptism. The media and a good part of Catholic opinion support ordination. However, given the current state of ordained ministry, this seems counterproductive to me. Can we seriously consider ordaining women when the ministry is so weakened and even called into question? Indeed, the French Independent Commission on Sexual Abuse in the Catholic Church (CIASE) has brought to light the "abuse" of sacredness conferred on the sacrament of holy orders. By what miracle could this be "of divine institution"?[4] We cannot help but see in this provision a maneuver toward self-legitimization by the clerical body. Also, it is better to hope that women do not become complicit in such an institution. This would be, as Pope Francis said, "clericalizing women." And if the pope did not extend his remark by promising to declericalize male priests, it is perhaps because he considered the task impossible.

More fruitful, undoubtedly, is the baptismal way. It is the one that Pope Francis chose, particularly in his decision to confer on seventy laypeople the right to vote at the Synod on Synodality. If we estimate the number of women selected at thirty-five, to which were added five nuns, we arrive at a total of around forty women who could vote, out of around four hundred voters in total, or 10 percent of the electorate. Still little, but this start was encouraging.

The baptism just mentioned is called, in an inclusive Church, to play an even stronger role now; it is the only way to lift the silent but powerful exclusions that structure the Church. Regarding the relationship between the laity and priests, it is not wrong to speak of mistreatment of the laity. We will measure its exclusionary effects from this definition given by John Paul II: the laity include "all Christians who are not members of the sacred order and of the religious state recognized by the Church" (*CL* 9). This purely negative definition means that those "who are not" can only think of themselves by subtraction; they are "less." Laypeople, especially if they are involved in the Church, can only imagine themselves, consciously or not, as small-footed clerics, drawn to this reference figure that is their only mirror.

Certainly, the ministerial priesthood has its essential purpose in the royal priesthood of all the faithful and is oriented toward it (*LG* 10). Cardinal Yves Congar also says in a powerful formula that "the people are the pleroma of the hierarchy."[5] Pope Francis recalled that "the laity are the protagonists of the Church and the world; we are called to serve them, not to use them."[6] However, this situation is unhealthy. We must not forget that the laity run the domestic church and must be able to "think for themselves" according to positive criteria to be defined not in a Roman office but in conjunction with it because of the qualifications of "priest, prophet, and king" conferred on them by their baptism.

John Paul II amplifies the unease by the strong reaffirmation of the difference "of nature and not of degree" (*CL* 22) between the clergy and the laity, already explained by canon 230 of the Code of Canon Law.[7] John Paul II states, "However, *the exercise of such tasks does not make Pastors of the lay faithful*: in fact, a person is not a minister simply in performing a task, but through sacramental ordination. Only the Sacrament of Orders gives the ordained minister a particular participation in the office of Christ, the Shepherd and Head, and in his Eternal Priesthood" (*CL* 23, emphasis original). This distinction itself raises questions, because it makes the sacrament "in itself" disconnected from the recipient. Doesn't the New Testament start from the charisms of the people and then define functions (Eph 4:11)? Would this distinction not invite, then, the invention of a particular (and temporary) ordination that allows those of the laity endowed with pastoral charisms to enjoy the fullness of the pastoral function?

These brief remarks lead us to believe that major upheavals are inevitable in the relationship between the laity and the clergy. Perhaps they will not be done with noise and thunder but in the discretion of everyday life, quietly allowing laypeople to take on responsibilities under the title of their baptism in parallel with the remaining clerics. This depends, however, on strongly revalorizing, under the common priesthood of the baptized, the identity of the laity and the modalities of their access to governance.

INCULTURATION FOR TODAY'S WORLD

The other path to useful reform is for the Church to learn to listen to the world in which it lives. Certainly, the Church holds treasures that deserve to be listened to "religiously" for the word of God that they deliver. But the opposite is also necessary, and the current Church no longer knows how to understand or speak the language of common people. There too, tragedy invites itself. After centuries in which the Church lived to the rhythm of the society that surrounded it, it has recently been "exculturated," according to the word used by Danièle Hervieu-Léger, as it has distanced itself from its secular counterpart. If the Church wants to survive, it will have to re-inculturate itself. This may be a difficult task when we remember our past resistance to "speaking the culture" of Africans or Chinese. But here again is an essential task, both out of respect for the sense of faith (*sensus fidei*) of every follower of Christ[8] and because today's spiritual expectations are intense. Just as Jesus had pity on the crowds who had no shepherd (Matt 9:36–38), every baptized person must hear the deep dismay of their brothers and sisters faced with loss of all reference to anything greater than themselves, loss of the meaning of life, vulnerability in the face of a consumer society, an increase in violence, desensitization in the face of lies....Poverty today is no less demanding than yesterday!

To listen, debate, preach, and invite to pray, the Church must resolutely commit to an *aggiornamento* of its language by involving theologians and the faithful. How many Catholics say the Creed by wondering, often with fear, about the strange universe into which they have entered? This occurs also with the question of spirituality. The Church's considerable heritage has become almost unusable. For example, what does, this apparently simple formula: "to experience God" mean? In this matter, which is so fundamental and the subject of so many expectations, the Church can only move forward in a credible manner in conjunction with professionals in the human sciences, in particular psychologists. In doing so, the Church will be able to restore credibility to its spiritual heritage and consider establishing, perhaps within the framework of a "listening ministry," which already exists without having the name, a way to support people in search of meaning or wishing to reread their life journeys.

In this great task of inculturation, the Church is fortunate to be able to rely on its illustrious elders who, during the first centuries of Christianity, accomplished admirable work. Christian theologians, translators, and philosophers made their scriptures, their still nascent theology, their conception of morality and public life known to the Greco-Roman world. With impressive energy, they conversed with the thinkers of their time: Neoplatonists, followers of oriental cults or traditional Roman religion, and even resolute atheists. In short, they "communicated the risen Christ" in their cultural environment; they announced the good news. Their situation as a minority religion, deprived of power and even mistreated by it, had pruned their thinking and reinforced their arguments. If they debated well, it was because they were at the level of human beings, without an institutional overhang that grants itself the last word. This precedent invites Catholics, in France at least, not to fear becoming a minority again, because their Church could be better off for it, provided, of course, that it wishes to dialogue with today's culture.

Inculturation also means that the universalism of the Church does not depend on the uniformity of disciplines, which includes, for example, the celibacy of priests. What is valid in Madrid or Munich may not be valid in Seoul. However, the wind in Rome has not blown in this direction, until now. John Paul II's decision to reduce the powers of the National Episcopal Conferences by requiring the unanimity of voters increased Roman centralization and paralyzed decentralized initiatives.[9] Conversely, in *Evangelii Gaudium*, Pope Francis had considered giving more power to national and/or continental conferences.[10] No doubt he wanted to move forward in this direction during the Amazon Synod in 2019, but the decisions taken were minimal. Inculturation would be much more effective if decisions were taken closer to the beneficiaries, but for the moment, Rome is keeping control, even leaving doubt about its true intention for bringing into debate matters as decisive as its mode of governance, the sacredness of the priesthood, and priests' state of life.

Another reality is beginning to impose itself on European Catholics. African, Asian, and South American churches reflect other cultures and are not always affected by the same problems as Europeans. However, their influence on the course of the Church is expanding, diminishing European dominance. As of November 2024, there were sixty-four European and North American elector cardinals, compared to fifty-seven from the rest of the world.[11] These observations can destabilize common Western opinion, which, for its part, feels the need for in-depth reform. Why reform, if the clerical structure satisfies much of the world? This question raises two objections. The first is that the situation of Europe and North America, living in postmodernity, will undoubtedly be that of Africa and Asia tomorrow. The second is that, if we do not want to lose the majority of European or North American Catholics, their churches must adopt reforms that, in their context, are essential.

These observations question the capacity of the Church to reform itself. We don't often see a body that holds all the power in its own hands reforming of its own accord! Very often, an institution hopes to reform or lets us believe it is doing so but does not go deep enough in eradicating the problems. Many observers believe that the entanglement of Catholicism and clericalism is too old and too multifaceted to be eradicated. They hold that the institution has become so fragile, therefore so rigid, that it would be preferable to let it decline in peace and disappear. This opinion, which I have often verified to be that of very fine minds, leaves me with too much dissatisfaction not to try to temper it. Indeed, Christianity cannot be reborn from the dust that springs from a book that has been closed for many moons but must be transmitted face to face. And only a few individuals are needed, which is the fate of current Catholics. I conclude that we must accept what falls to our generation—the task of accompanying a painful, almost desperate transition, but where, precisely, hope can take shape. In short, within this uncomfortable tension, we must do everything possible so that the patient heals, while knowing that the patient may possibly disappear.

But if we think about it, what disappearance do we fear? If it is that of the institution, is that a problem? Let us recognize that some Catholics view that disappearance with concern. Yet isn't the institution, as François Cassingéna-Trevedy says, "decoration," which he recognizes is dying?[12] On the other hand, the Church of Christ is a much larger body whose limits no one knows. One Church can obscure another....The mortal Church institution must not hide the Church of Christ, which is far beyond the limits we see.

THE PURPOSES OF THE CHURCH

To become more visible, this Church of Christ, whether taking shape behind the institution or being prepared in the secret of the time to come, has its own objectives and ends. Certainly, these ends are known and often practiced and taught. But two risks, reinforced under the onslaught of current storms, threaten the Church. The first is to absolutize the means, the institution; the second is that the object seems too distant or too inaccessible to energize the existence of the Church. On the Catholic stage today, the first temptation is easy to spot. How many tearful laments about the lack of priests, how many calls to "save the Church," how many freeze-frames praising a so-called eternal past whose aim is to enshrine its current structure, how many injunctions on unity and especially on the duty of obedience have we witnessed? Faced with this defensive arsenal, we can only verify that the current attachment to the institutional structure is excessive, almost idolatrous. In addition, it dries up the Church and converts it into a technocracy. The second risk is to postpone the question of the Church's purpose to the end of history, denying it has any immediate value. But this is an offense against the faith. When the first Christians greeted each other with the formula "Maranatha," "The Lord is coming," they were not thinking of the end of time but were already enjoying his presence in their midst. By saying this to each other so frequently, they were already working to accomplish it. Finally, it is lack of vision that promotes division, in this case between reformers and conservatives, because we no longer look in the same direction together.

It is therefore worth recalling what the ends of the Church are. The Church does not exist for itself, nor does it look to itself; it follows a star. As the wise men followed "the star at its rising," the Church, too, is attracted to the star, seeking to rejoice in its light and beauty. Thus, the Church must be in continuous movement toward its end, which is the contemplation of the promised Savior. The Church is not the center, neither in self-satisfaction nor in remorse, but moves toward the one who gives the Church its reason for being, therefore its end. Permanent movement, incessant contemplation...reforming without reflection on the end would make the Church an ordinary communication enterprise. Deadly, nothing more.

The ends of the Church are three in number: to announce "good news," to bring about a kingdom that is both here and yet to come, and to obey the commandment of love recalled by Jesus. A little weariness arises at the utterance of these words, which have become dull as they have been used and abused. For our contemporaries, is the "good news" today more than the promise of a free packet of cookies? By questioning the word itself, let's try to put some pink back into its cheeks. What is it, if not what its sender promises and what its recipient wants to do with it? To know the promise of the sender, remember that the word is the translation of the Greek *euangelion* and allow the profusion of evangelical stories to arise before you: Jesus, his life given, his saving passion, and his remarkable resurrection that expands time to the infinity of God. But the word only fulfills its performative vocation if the recipient hears that the good news is always...new. Every morning, we will find something new there, if we are attentive to what bursts into our existence and covers it with its energizing shadow until we become one with it.

Looking at society, this supposes that the good news walks in step with the world around it, which does not mean that it blends in but that it must understand the world's words, its culture, and its mechanisms, instead of letting itself be tempted by a countercultural stance that would be its own fortress. For the world, the good news must become a star and be a watchman in the outposts, not at the rear. This is what the Bible suggests to the people of Israel. In a circumstance where dangers were accumulating, God asks Jeremiah what he sees, and the prophet replies, "I see a branch of 'watchman'" (Jer 1:11–12, Jerusalem Bible), a name that also designates the almond tree, the first tree to flower at the beginning of spring. This is how the prophetic vocation of the Church is defined: it announces life, in season and out of season. There is no Church without an assumed and effective prophetic dimension. However, institutions only agree with prophets who do not anger them; the others they push to the margins, ignoring them or silencing them.

But the good news goes beyond the immediate course of days. In the Christian realm, it crystallizes around the announcement of the resurrection of Jesus. But, in the daily life of parishes, in the work of theologians, and even in the magisterium, the discourse on the resurrection has dried up over the last one or two generations. Undoubtedly a consequence of the positivist current dominant in the nineteenth century, this impoverishment comes from the fact that the "how" of the resurrection took precedence over the announcement itself. Now, venturing to answer the question "How will we be resurrected?" locks us into a dead end. As long as we confuse "resurrection of the flesh" (designating the identity of a subject and not "meat") and resurrection of the body, the trap closes. Would the flesh return to our bones, as Ezekiel's vision reminds us? How ridiculous! No, the subject of resurrection is something else entirely. The dialogue between Jesus and Martha reveals the heart of it: "I am the resurrection and the life. Those who believe in me, even though they die, will live, and everyone who lives and believes in me will never die." And Martha replied: "Yes, Lord, I believe that you are the Messiah, the Son of God, the one coming into the world" (John 11:25–27).

These words show that resurrection is born of faith in Christ, that faith is the fire that invigorates existence. And this extra life is the promise of eternity. This means, on the one hand, that this faith makes us live today in a fullness that goes beyond anything we can imagine and, on the other hand, that faith, again, overflows the present life and exceeds it, to the point of leading the human being to the shores of a "life without decline," about which we know nothing except that faith promises it to us. This confidence in a future that is always open but totally sealed in the hands of God seems to be fading. A large percentage of Catholics, if you listen to the polls, do not believe in the resurrection; for them, physical death is a term that is difficult to overcome. And faced with the aporia of "how" to which they have had to submit, they prefer to remain silent.

But if the Church no longer announces the resurrection of Christ, the premise of our resurrection, our hope is vain because faith in this resurrection, undefinable but certain, nourishes hope. Consequently, if the Church wants to reform, it must first reconnect with a vigorous, ardent, and well-argued proclamation of the resurrection. The Church must also prove in its daily actions that the risen one is present, both within it and in the world, not using it to gain power, but to serve. In short, it must honor Bossuet's formula: "The Church is Jesus Christ spread and communicated."

The next purpose of the Church is to announce a kingdom of which Christ is king, and that straddles the present and the future. Already here and not yet. A very real kingdom, woven from the minutiae of ordinary life that makes kindness, love, and solidarity grow. But a kingdom in the making, always in the future, greater and richer than what is visible; such an announcement is considerably dynamic. Here we find an awareness of time, without which no project is possible, a fair and modest estimation of oneself (one actor among others), and a strong solidarity with future generations. Proclaiming the kingdom means building a bridge from the present to the future. In addition, the image carries with it a good dose of enthusiasm and of invitation to create, following the Creator God. Announcing the kingdom is welcoming the slight imbalance that pushes us forward in the conviction that our citizenship, if it begins here on earth, is also called to be celestial. Faithful followers of Christ deserve to be told about the future. It's even their right. What will their parish, their diocese, the whole Church be in thirty years? With which actors? For which company? What about the person that dies tomorrow? How will the Church's end have been realized?

Finally, the commandment of love is imposed upon the followers of Christ, reaffirmed by Jesus to the Pharisees: "You shall love the Lord your God with all your heart, and with all your soul, and with all your mind." And: "You shall love your neighbor as yourself" (Matt 22:37–39). Here again, the word *love* is perilous to use as counterfeits have worn it out so much. This is why it is perhaps easier to understand by hearing again what the prophet Isaiah attributed to God: "You are precious in my sight,...and I love you" (Isa 43:4), because this word recognizes God's initiative in having loved first. Christians can know a little better how to love if they can look at how God loves. They see love in the way Jesus taught, welcomed, freed bodies from their illnesses, and relieved spirits from their demons. They see it at the cross, where Jesus, "having loved his own...loved them to the end" (John 13:1). The cross—the place of life given, of forgiveness always offered, of evil vanquished, and of humanity gathered from an innocent man condemned to the most infamous torture. Consequently, he who gives, forgives, frees, and embraces the most rejected—he knows how to love. Today, the key attitude toward others is to announce to them, by inventing the appropriate gestures and words, that they are valuable in the eyes of God and that they are loved. Yes, as Christiane Singer reminded us, love is "the very essence of the world."[13] This means that without love, however imperfect, however suspect of diverted intentions, the world does not stand up; it descends into violence. The Church has no message more beautiful to deliver than this urgency to love.

These, then, are the three ends, the three pillars rooted in fire, that will remain whatever institution adopts them: announcing the death and resurrection of Jesus Christ, energizing existence by preaching a kingdom already here, and finding its center in a love offered to all, freely, without merit, "because it is him."

At the end of this journey, and within its limits, I am reminded of the long lamentations of the prophet before the lost temple, during the fall of Jerusalem (587 BCE): "Our hearts are sick,...our eyes have grown dim....But you, O LORD, reign for ever; your throne endures to all generations" (Lam 5:17, 19). What does the prophet ask, if not to maintain trust in God? I would like to evoke this spirit of one who trusts in divine wisdom without fear. May the seed thrown onto the ground or the road that turns into dust be our hope. May the christic purpose of the Church, purified and sparkling, emerge from the obsolescence of its structure. Can we imagine that "the heart of Christianity is only beginning to beat"?[14] In this journey toward the hidden Church, the Gospel is our viaticum, our true treasure. Nothing else, then, is more important than giving Christ our flesh so that he can advance with us on new paths.

NOTES

CHAPTER 1

1. L. Manicardi, *La passione per l'umano* (Vita e Pensiero, 2023), 128.

2. Conference of Scandinavian Bishops, Letter on Human Sexuality, March 25, 2023.

3. Martin Buber, *Eclipse of God: Studies in the Relation between Religion and Philosophy* ([1952] Princeton University Press, 2016), 73.

CHAPTER 2

1. La Conférence des religieux et religieuses de France (CORREF), *Groupes de Travail CORREF Post Ciase, préconisations et guide de bonnes pratiques*, April 14, 2023, https://www.viereligieuse.fr/groupes-de-travail-corref-post-ciase-preconisations-et-guide-de-bonnes-pratiques/.

2. See the remarkable investigation by Céline Hoyeau, *La trahison des pères* (Bayard, 2021).

3. Philippe Lefebvre, *Comment tuer Jésus? abus, violences et emprises dans la Bible* (Cerf, 2021).

4. CORREF.

CHAPTER 3

1. Francis, *Spiritus Domini* [Modifying Canon 230 sec. 1 of the Code of Canon Law Regarding Access of Women to the Ministries of Lector and Acolyte], The Holy See, January 10, 2021.

2. To gauge the extent of work on this question, see in particular Bernard Pottier, *Le diaconat féminin, jadis et bientôt* (Lessius, 2021); Phyllis Zagano, "Survey of Vatican Studies on the Diaconate of Women," *Theological Studies* (September 2024). On the question of the "representation" of Christ that would require the presence of a man, see Phyllis Zagano, *Women: Icons of Christ* (Paulist Press, 2020).

3. The text published following the Synod for Amazonia made strong reference to the place of women in the life of Amazonian communities. As a result, in sec. 102 it asked that an instituted ministry of "the woman community leader" be created and recognized to serve the changing demands of evangelization and community service. See *Document final du synode des évêques pour l'Amazonie* (Lessius, 2020), 99–103, as well as card 13, "Ministères féminins" of this edition commented on by the Jesuits of Ceras. At the second session of the Synod on Synodality, the prospect of women being ordained to the diaconate receded once again.

4. Not to masculinize, in this case not to clericalize women: this theme is associated with the concern to "demasculinize the Church," expressed several times by Pope Francis. But wouldn't the primary objective be to "declericalize" the office of priest and pastoral responsibility?

5. Lauriane Savoy, *Pionnières. Comment les femmes sont devenues pasteures* (Labor et Fides, 2023).

6. See H-U von Balthasar and the revival of his theme by John Paul II, *MD*, 27, note 5.

7. See Michel Quesnel, *Paul et les femmes. Ce qu'il a écrit, ce qu'on lui a fait dire* (Médiaspaul, 2021), 52–56.

8. See François Marxer, *Au péril de la nuit. Femmes mystiques du 20ème siècle* (Cerf, 2017). We also refer to chapter 5 of our book *L'Eglise, des femmes avec des hommes* (Cerf, 2019), 192–240, which mentions some "Eclats du féminin," suggesting a more feminine style.

CHAPTER 4

1. When we speak of the Church, we are referring to the Catholic Church, unless otherwise stated.

2. Independent Commission on Sexual Abuse in the Church. All published documents are available on its website https://www.ciase.fr/.

3. The rise in power began in the 1970s and 1980s. See Marie-Jo Thiel, *L'Église catholique face aux abus sexuels sur mineurs* (Bayard, 2019), chapter 1.

4. See Marie-Jo Thiel, *Plus fort, car vulnérable! Quand la vulnérabilité interroge la crise des abus dans l'Église*, with contributions by Patrick Goujon (Salvator, 2023).

5. Marie-Jo Thiel, "Le visage de l'Église de France sous le projecteur de la Covid-19," *E.T.-Studies* 12, no. 1 (2021): 51–64.

6. Jacques Bernard, "Le Saliah: de Moïse à Jésus Christ et de Jésus Christ aux Apôtres," in *La vie de la Parole: de l'Ancien au Nouveau Testament: études d'exégèse et d'herméneutique bibliques offertes à Pierre Grelot, professeur à l'Institut catholique de Paris*, Département des études bibliques de l'Institut catholique de Paris (Desclée, 1987), 409–20.

7. Jean-Bernard Livio, "Why Were Women the First to Go to the Tomb," *Cath.ch* (April 7, 2023). Unfortunately, Pope Gregory the Great, in a 591 sermon, mixed up different types of "Mary Magdalene, capable of uniting in herself forgiveness and reconciliation" by "removing her role as a disciple and confining her to that of a repentant sinner," emphasizing God's mercy. It was only Paul VI, who at the end of the 1960s removed the readings from the liturgy that focused on the "sinner" and rehabilitated this figure. Pope Francis in 2016 recommended that she be given the title, still retained in Eastern tradition, "Apostle of the Apostles."

8. Françoise Héritier, *Masculin/Féminin II. Dissoudre la hiérarchie* (Odile Jacob, 2002), 18.

9. M. Dujarier, "Redécouvrons la théologie du Christ-frère," in *Le défi de la fraternité. Die Herausforderung der Geschwisterlichkeit*, ed. Marie-Jo Thiel and Marc Feix (Lit Verlag, 2018), 281–92.

10. See, for example, chapter 2 of Luca Castiglioni, *Filles et fils de Dieu. Égalité baptismale et différence sexuelle* (Cerf, 2020). Or

see the works of Anne-Marie Pelletier, *L'Église et le féminin. Revisiter l'histoire pour servir l'Évangile* (Salvator, 2021), or *L'Église des femmes avec des hommes* (Cerf, 2019).

11. Mary E. Hunt, "Be Not Ordained: Move beyond the Same Old Song and Dance on Women's Ordination," *National Catholic Reporter* (April 3, 2023). This is also the view of Jean-François Chiron, "L'argumentation du pape François a sa valeur…et ses limites," *La Croix* (December 3, 2022).

12. Christoph Theobald, "Le concile Vatican II face à l'inconnu. L'aventure d'un discernement collégial des 'signes des temps,'" *Études 417*, no. 10 (2012): 354. His quotations from John XXIII come from John XXIII and Paul VI, *Addresses to the Council* (Ed. Centurion, 1966), 27ff.

13. See Gerhard Kruip, "Le chemin synodal en Allemagne. Un pas vers la réforme de l'Église?," in *Abus sexuels: écouter, enquêter, prévenir*, ed. Marie-Jo Thiel, Anne Danion-Grilliat, and Frédéric Trautmann (Strasbourg University Press, Coll. Chemins d'Éthique, 2022), 385–98; and Gerhard Kruip, "Les abus sexuels, un problème systémique pour l'Église," in *S'aventurer en éthique. Hommage à Marie-Jo Thiel*, ed. Talitha Cooreman-Guittin and Frédéric Trautmann (Strasbourg University Press, coll. Chemins d'éthique, 2022), 189–97.

14. The interdisciplinary report on paedocriminality in Germany was entrusted to researchers from the universities of Mannheim, Heidelberg, and Gießen (hence the acronym MHG). Led by Harald Dressing, the study group worked from July 1, 2014, to September 24, 2018, using data provided by twenty-seven German dioceses.

15. Der Synodale Weg, *Orientierungstext. Auf dem Weg der Umkehr und der Erneuerung. Theologische Grundlagen des Synodalen Weges der katholischen Kirche in Deutschland.* Adopted by the Synodal Assembly on February 3, 2022, 41.

16. See Luca Castiglioni, *Filles et fils de Dieu*, 181–233.

17. Mission de France, reported in Conférence des évêques de France, *Collecte des synthèses synodales* (June 9, 2022), 6. Emphasis added.

18. This applies to other continents: for example, the *North American Final Document for the Continental Stage of the 2021–2024 Synod, For a Synodal Church: Communion, Participation and*

Mission, 19, p. 9. See also Loup Besmond de Senneville, "Ce que les catholiques du monde entier ont voulu dire à Rome, " *La Croix* (April 24, 2023).

19. Der Synodale Weg, *Grundtext. Frauen in Diensten und Ämtern in der Kirche, SW5* (Sekretariat des Synodalen Weges, Bonn, 2022). Adopted by the Synodal Assembly in its fifth session on September 9, 2022. Author's translation. In autumn 2022, however, it was necessary to merge three action texts on the subject of women into one. Thanks to Margit Eckholt (email April 13, 2023) for her explanations.

20. Domination of a master, *kyrios* (3.3, p. 23).

21. See Marie-Jo Thiel, *La grâce et la pesanteur. Le célibat obligatoire des prêtres en question* (DDB, 2024).

22. The ecumenical aspect is dealt with in 5.4, p. 61 ff.

23. The German concept of *Menschliche Natur* translates the idea of human nature beyond the masculine/feminine. The Johannine Prologue could also be added to the synod's argument: "The Word became flesh" does not mean that Christ became masculine but that he took on human flesh. Christ's masculinity is only a variation of Christ's humanity, which is the central point of the incarnation.

24. Margit Eckholt, email of April 13, 2023. ZdK is the Zentralkomitee der deutschen Katholiken (Central Committee of German Catholics). It is the official body representing laypeople within the Roman Catholic Church in Germany. It comprises representatives of various Catholic organizations.

25. Francis, *Querida Amazonia* [Dear Amazonia], The Holy See (February 2, 2020), 100–101.

26. Margit Eckholt and Johanna Rahner, eds., *Christusrepräsentanz. Zur aktuellen Debatte um die Zulassung von Frauen zum priesterlichen Amt* (Herder, 2021).

27. Florent Guénard, *La Passion de l'égalité* (Seuil, 2022), 14.

28. Guénard, *La Passion de l'égalité*, 278.

29. "If I had been a boy…, I think I would have wanted to be a priest." Quoted in Claude Langlois, *La femme du Seigneur. Madeleine Delbrêl en ses œuvres* (Cerf, 2022), 299.

30. Der Synodale Weg, *Grundtext*, 64.

31. Philippa Rath, ed., *"Weil Gott es so will." Frauen erzählen von ihrer Berufung zur Diakonin und Priesterin* (Herder, 2021), 19, 11.

32. Der Synodale Weg, *Grundtext*, 66.

33. Der Synodale Weg, *Grundtext*, 68.

34. Der Synodale Weg, *Grundtext*, 69.

35. Interview with Cardinal Jean-Claude Hollerich by Andrea Tornielli, *Vatican News*, April 27, 2023.

36. Céline Béraud (sociologist), "Parmi les évêques, certains ont encore du mal à reconnaître l'existence du caractère systémique des abus," *Le Monde*, April 14, 2023.

37. See Saint Gregory the Great, *Homélies sur Ézéchiel, I*, Homélie 7, n. 8 and 9, trans. Charles Morel, Sources chrétiennes no. 327 (Cerf, 1986), 245–47.

38. Yves-Marie Blanchard, *Contre le cléricalisme, retour à l'Évangile* (Salvator, 2023), 113.

CHAPTER 5

1. Francis, Christmas Greetings to the Roman Curia, December 21, 2015, https://www.vatican.va/content/francesco/en/speeches/2015/december/documents/papa-francesco_20151221_curia-romana.html#.

2. Francis, Christmas Greetings to the Roman Curia, December 22, 2016, https://www.vatican.va/content/francesco/en/speeches/2016/december/documents/papa-francesco_20161222_curia-romana.html.

3. Francis, Christmas Greetings to the Roman Curia, December 21, 2015.

4. Francis, Christmas Greetings to the Roman Curia, December 22, 2016.

5. Francis, Christmas Greetings to the Roman Curia, December 22, 2016.

6. Francis, Christmas Greetings to the Roman Curia, December 21, 2017, https://www.vatican.va/content/francesco/en/events/event.dir.html/content/vaticanevents/en/2017/12/21/curia-romana.html.

7. Francis, Christmas Greetings to the Roman Curia, December 21, 2019, https://www.vatican.va/content/francesco/en/speeches/2019/december/documents/papa-francesco_20191221_curia-romana.html.

8. Francis, Christmas Greetings to the Roman Curia, December 22, 2016.

9. In his December 21, 2019, address, Pope Francis once again clarified that the missionary dimension is at the heart of this reform, echoing his words from *Evangelii Gaudium*: "The renewal of structures demanded by pastoral conversion can only be understood in this light: as part of an effort to make them more mission-oriented" (27).

10. J. Famérée, "*Sensus fidei, sensus fidelium*—histoire d'une notion théologique discutée," *Recherches de science religieuse* 2 (2016): 167.

11. ITC, "The *Sensus Fidei* in the Life of the Church," 2014, 23, https://www.vatican.va/roman_curia/congregations/cfaith/cti_documents/rc_cti_20140610_sensus-fidei_en.html.

12. Vincent de Lérins, *Commonitorium*, II, 5; Corpus Christianorum: Series Latina 64, 149; quoted by Famérée, "*Sensus fidei, sensus fidelium*," 170.

13. For a more detailed historical account that goes beyond our current discussion and the distinctions between the different categories of *sensus fidei*, refer to ITC, "The *Sensus Fidei* in the Life of the Church."

14. Paul VI, *Presbyterorum Ordinis* (On the Ministry and Life of Priests), The Holy See, December 7, 1965, 9, https://www.vatican.va/archive/hist_councils/ii_vatican_council/documents/vat-ii_decree_19651207_presbyterorum-ordinis_en.html.

15. ITC, "The *Sensus Fidei* in the Life of the Church," 3.

16. Francis, Address to the Members of the International Theological Commission, December 5, 2014.

17. J.- M. Bergoglio, *Meditaciones para religiosos* (San Miguel, 1982), 46–47; quoted by S.-T. Bonino, "Pour lire le document: le *Sensus fidei* dans la vie de l'Église," 2014, I–1.

18. Francis, "Address for the Conclusion of the Third Extraordinary General Assembly of the Synod of Bishops," October 18, 2014.

19. Secretariat of the Synod of Bishops, Preparatory Document for the Synod of Bishops "For a Synodal Church: Communion, Participation, and Mission," September 7, 2021.

CHAPTER 6

1. See "Diaconia 2013–2023: la dimension sociale de l'évangélisation," *Lumen Vitae* 78 (January-March 2023): 1.

2. Jean-Claude Caillaux, "'Place et parole des pauvres,' un groupe source et moteur," *Cahiers de l'Atelier* 540, "Poursuivre l'élan de Diaconia" (January-March 2014): 20.

3. The Independent Commission on Sexual Abuse in the Church (CIASE), also known as the Sauvé Commission, is a French commission of inquiry created on February 8, 2019, and led by Jean-Marc Sauvé. In its 2,500-page report issued on October 5, 2021, it established the facts on sexual abuse of minors and vulnerable persons in the Catholic Church in France since the 1950s.

4. Étienne Grieu, *Le Dieu qui ne compte pas. À l'écoute des humiliés et des boiteux* (Salvator, 2023), especially chapter 2, "L'Évangile de 'ceux qui ne comptent pas,'" 29–44.

5. Laure Blanchon, "Le trésor caché dans les marges," *Christus* 259: "Décentrés pour aimer. Vers les périphéries" (July 2018): 23.

6. See Conférence des évêques de France, Collecte des synthèses diocésaines pour le synode 2021–2024 sur la synodalité, 3. English version: https://eglise.catholique.fr/wp-content/uploads/sites/2/2022/07/National-Synthesis-Document-French-episcopal-Conference-june-2022.pdf.

7. See François Odinet, "L'Église réformée par ses 'périphéries,'" *Études* 4291 (March 2022): 67–77.

8. See Frédéric-Marie Le Méhauté, *Révélé aux tout-petits. Une théologie à l'écoute des plus pauvres*, Cogitatio fidei 317 (Cerf, 2022), 89–140.

9. Francis, Speech during the Ecumenical Meeting, Riga, September 24, 2018; and Francis, *Fratelli tutti* (On Fraternity and Social Friendship), The Holy See, October 3, 2020, 277.

10. As shown, for example, in the life stories of the program *Parole de vie / Word of Life* radio broadcast on RCF Mediterranean. See also Étienne Grieu, Gwennola Rimbaut, and Laure Blanchon,

eds., *Qu'est-ce qui fait vivre encore quand tout s'écroule? Une théologie à l'école des plus pauvres* (Lumen Vitae, 2017).

11. Laure Blanchon, *Récits de vie des plus pauvres, parole de vie pour tous* (Salvator/ Éditions franciscaines, 2017), 144.

12. Marie-José Perdoux, *Parole de vie / Word of Life*, RCF Mediterranean, 2001, radio program.

13. For example: the program *Parole de vie / Word of Life* broadcast on RCF Mediterranean in connection with the Diaconia of the Diocese of Var, life stories developed at the Sappel as part of the year of mercy, life stories collected by groups of the Saint-Laurent Network during celebrations and gatherings, and training to become actors-witnesses organized by Caritas.

14. Laure Blanchon, *Récits de vie des plus pauvres, parole de vie pour tous*, 114–15.

15. François Odinet, "Les 'véritables dimensions' de la résurrection," *Nouvelle revue théologique* 144 (2022): 541–58.

16. I note these few points from my engagement with people in very precarious situations with *La Pierre d'Angle* (*The Corner Stone*, an association of Fourth World people and people in covenant with them, sharing the Gospel and fraternity; this association is part of the Saint-Laurent Network), and from my work in a research seminar at Loyola Paris Faculties "Au creux du malheur, la lumière? À l'écoute de ceux qui passent par le gouffre?" (2018–2022), which ended in January 2023 with a symposium published by Laure Blanchon, Christophe Pichon, and Jean-Claude Caillaux, *Au creux du malheur, la lumière? À l'écoute de ceux qui passent par le gouffre?* (Lumen Vitae, 2024).

17. Charlotte, *Parole de vie / Word of Life*, RCF Mediterranean, November 2001, radio program.

18. According to the research work carried out between people in precarious situations and theologians by the Working Group in Dialogue with the Poorest, Loyola Paris Faculties 2022–2023, based on the question: "When Jesus tells us: 'I am with you every day,' what does that mean when there is misfortune/misery?" Research published in *Séminaire dialogal. Une traversée. Dieu présent dans le Malheur?* (Éditions Aquiprint, 2023).

19. See Frédéric-Marie Le Méhauté, *Révélé aux tout-petits. Une théologie à l'écoute des plus pauvres*, 233–89.

20. Francis, Speech to the Pilgrims of the Siloe Group, Rome, July 6, 2016. Siloe is a collective of associations engaged with the very poor and living the Gospel in the spirituality of Father Joseph Wresinski. https://www.vatican.va/content/francesco/en/speeches/2016/july/documents/papa-francesco_20160706_poveri-diocesi-lyon.pdf. The exact quote is: "In the heart of the Church, you allow us to meet Jesus, because you speak to us about him, not so much with words, but with your whole life."

21. Francis, Speech to the Pilgrims of the Siloe Group. The exact quote is: "Together with the caregivers who are accompanying you, you offer a beautiful testimony of evangelical fraternity in walking together on the pilgrimage. You have indeed come accompanying one another. The caregivers have generously helped you, by providing resources and time to enable you to come; and you, you give to them, you give to us, you give to me, Jesus himself."

22. As Philippe Ottavis says, for example, when recounting feeling anonymous, *Parole de vie / Word of life* (undated), RCF Mediterranean, radio program.

23. Laure Blanchon, "Ces liens qui font vivre," in Etienne Grieu, Gwennola Rimbaut, Laure Blanchon, eds., *Qu'est-ce qui fait vivre encore quand tout s'écroule? Une théologie à l'école des plus pauvres*, 55–80.

24. Numerous testimonies from *Parole de vie / Words of Life*, broadcast on RCF Mediterranean, echo this dynamic.

CHAPTER 7

1. 2013–2014.

2. Elisabeth Schussler Fiorenza, Mary Daly, Kari Elisabeth Børresen, Yvonne Pellé-Douël, Marie-Jeanne Bérère, Donna Singles, the Women and Ministries and L'autre parole movements, in Quebec, Women and Men in the Church, and so many others.

3. The Skirt Committee, born in 2008; Christine Pedotti and Anne Soupa, *Feet in the Font* (Presses de la Renaissance, 2010); Anne Soupa, *Does God Love Women?* (Médiaspaul, 2012).

4. Code of Canon Law, c. 1008, in *The Code of Canon Law: Latin-English Edition* (Canon Law Society of America, 1983).

5. Yves Congar, *Milestones for a Theology of the Laity* (Cerf, 1952), coll. "Unam Sanctam" 32, p. 642.

6. Francis, Letter to Cardinal Marc Ouellet, March 19, 2016.

7. *Code of Canon Law*, c. 230: "When the necessity of the Church warrants it and when ministers are lacking, lay persons, even if they are not lectors or acolytes, can also supply for certain of their offices, namely, to exercise the ministry of the word, to preside over liturgical prayers, to confer Baptism, and to distribute Holy Communion in accord with the prescriptions of the law."

8. The meaning of faith is already attested in the New Testament. 1 John 2:20, 27 says, "But you have been anointed by the Holy One, and all of you have knowledge....You do not need anyone to teach you."

9. John Paul II, *Apostolos Suos* (Apostolic Letter on the Theological and Juridical Nature of Episcopal Conferences), The Holy See, May 21, 1998, 22, https://www.vatican.va/. Section 22 requires unanimity for decisions that come under an authentic magisterium (in doctrinal matters), unless recognized by the Holy See, which would require a qualified majority.

10. Pope Francis recalled this on October 17, 2015, in these terms: "In a synodal Church, as I have already stated, 'it is not appropriate for the pope to replace the local episcopates in the discernment of all the problems that arise in their territories. In this sense, I feel the need to progress in a beneficial 'decentralization'" (*EG*, secs. 16, 32).

11. Holy See Press Office, https://press.vatican.va/content/salastampa/en/documentation/cardinali---statistiche/composizione-per-area.html.

12. François Cassingéna-Trevedy, "Le 'décor' du Christianisme est mort, son coeur commence seulement de battre," *Zeteo*, podcast, May 13, 2023, https://www.zeteo.fr/post/fran%C3%A7ois-cassing%C3%A9na-le-d%C3%A9cor-du-christianisme-est-mort-son-coeur-commence-seulement-de-battre.

13. Christiane Singer, "Derniers fragments d'un long voyage" (Albin Michel, 2007).

14. Cassingena-Trévedy, "Le 'décor' du Christianisme est mort."

ABOUT THE AUTHORS

Laure Blanchon, Ursuline sister of the Roman Union, is a doctor of theology and professor of dogmatic and practical theology at the Facultés Loyola Paris. She has published *Récits de vie des plus pauvres, Paroles de vie pour tous* (Éditions franciscaines/Salvator, 2017), *Voici les noces de l'Agneau. Quand l'incarnation passe par les pauvres* (Lessius, 2017), and *Au creux du malheur, la lumière? À l'écoute de ceux qui passent par le gouffre* (with Jean-Claude Caillaux and Christophe Pichon, at Éditions jésuites, 2024). She contributed to *Witnesses of Synodality, Good Practices and Experiences* (edited by Jos Moons, Paulist Press, 2024).

Isabelle de La Garanderie, consecrated virgin of the diocese of Nanterre, is a graduate in French literature and in dogmatic theology. She is a PhD student in theology and teaches French in a disadvantaged area. She has published *La réconciliation—chemin d'initiation et de croissance ecclésiales* (CLD/NRT, 2020), *Membres d'un même corps* (Artège, 2022), and has contributed to *Il a donné pouvoir à ses serviteurs—cinq regards de femmes sur la gouvernance dans l'Église* (Emmanuel, 2024).

Véronique Margron, provincial prioress of the Dominican Sisters of Charity of the Presentation and moral theologian, is president of the Conference of Religious Men and Women of France and former dean of the faculty of theology at the Catholic University of the West in Angers. She has published *Un moment de verité* with Jérôme Cordelier (Albin Michel, 2019).

Anne-Marie Pelletier is Professor Emeritus of Literature of the Universités de Paris-X et Gustave Eiffel, a doctor of religious science, and a recipient of the Ratzinger Award in 2014. She has devoted a large part of her work to questions of biblical hermeneutics (*D'âge en âge, les Ecritures*, Lessius, 2004). For several years she has also been reflecting on the feminine in the light of biblical revelation: *Le signe de la femme* (Cerf, 2006), *L'Eglise, des femmes avec des hommes* (Cerf, 2019), and *L'Eglise et le féminin* (Salvator, 2021).

Lucetta Scaraffia is an Italian historian and journalist, former director of the women's supplement of *L'Osservatore romano.* Ardent advocate of the role of women in the Church, she has authored numerous books, including *Du dernier Rang* (Salvator, 2016; 2nd ed. 2020), *La fin de la Mère* (Salvator, 2018), and the novel *Madame la cardinale* (Salvator, 2019).

Anne Soupa is a biblical scholar and writer and cofounder of the Skirt Committee and the Catholic Conference of French-Speaking Baptized People. She has published with Salvator *Douze femmes dans la vie de Jésus* (2014), *Le jour où Luther a dit non* (2017), and *Consoler les catholiques* (2019) and with Sylvaine Landrivon, *Marie telle que vous ne l'avez jamais vue* (2024). At Albin Michel, she has published *Judas le coupable idéal* (2018), *Pour l'amour de Dieu* (2021), and with Christine Pedotti, *Espérez!* (2022). *Galla Placidia, l'impératrice face aux grandes migrations* was published by Editions du Cerf (2025).

About the Authors

Marie-Jo Thiel, physician by training, is professor emeritus at the University of Strasbourg. Engaged in the field of abuse prevention in the Church, she has published several books on the subject, including *L'Église catholique face aux abus sexuels sur mineurs* (Bayard, 2019), *Abus sexuels: écouter, enquêter, prévenir* (Presses universitaires de Strasbourg, 2022), *Plus forts car vulnérables* (Salvator, 2023), and *La grâce et la pesanteur. Le célibat obligatoire des prêtres en question* (DDB, 2024).